SPITFIRE

OSPREY
PUBLISHING

SPITFIRE

THE LEGEND LIVES ON

By John Dibbs and Tony Holmes

DEDICATION

I'd like to dedicate this book to Norman Lees, a dearly missed friend, who encouraged and helped me navigate the subtleties and safe practices of aerial photo work in my early days. He was and is my guide.

John Dibbs

First published in Great Britain in 2016 by Osprey Publishing,
PO Box 883, Oxford, OX1 9PL, UK
1385 Broadway, 5th Floor, New York, NY 10018, USA
E-mail: info@ospreypublishing.com

Osprey Publishing, part of Bloomsbury Publishing Plc

ACKNOWLEDGEMENTS

The authors would like to thank Stephen Grey, Jane Larcombe and all at The
Fighter Collection, John Romain and all at the Aircraft Restoration Company
and Historic Flying Limited, Dan Friedkin at Comanche Warbirds, Peter
Monk and all at The Biggin Hill Heritage Hangar, Peter Teichman and his crew
at Hangar 11, Phill O'Dell and the Rolls-Royce Heritage Programme Team,
Thomas Kaplan and the late Simon Marsh at Mark One Partners LLC, Sarah
Hanna at The Old Flying Machine Company, Steve Barber and the SoCal
Wing CAF, Chris and Elaine Fairfax at Fairfax Spitfires LLP, Robs Lamplough,
Richard Lake and Ian Smith at Eastern Airways and Rudy Frasca and family
at the Frasca Air Museum.

Also, special thanks to Geoffrey Wellum for his Foreword and service, as
well as Phill O'Dell for the introduction and his service too.

Aviation photography is the result of much hard work and coordination,
and we are indebted to all the owners, operators, engineers and pilots
that made this book possible. Special thanks to the cameraship pilots too,
Tim Ellison, Richard Verrall, the late Norman Lees, 'Punch' Churchill, Andy
Hill and Will Gray.

We have relied heavily on Peter R. Arnold during the compilation of this
volume, both for photographs and information. His immense knowledge of
the Spitfire never ceases to amaze us, whilst his archive of photos has no
equal. Fellow aviation historians Norman Franks, Phil Jarrett, Kent Ramsey,
Wojtek Matusiak, Andy Saunders, Andy Thomas and Chris Thomas have
also provided key photographs and/or information for this book, as has
Chris Yeoman. Thanks also to Chris Fairfax, owner of Spitfire F VC EE602, for
allowing us to visit him and trawl through the aeroplane's document archive,
and to Neil Duncanson and Sarah Joyce of North One Television for the
provision of information and photographs relating to Spitfire F IA N3200.
Finally, thank you to Simon Watson and Justin Sawyer at The Aviation
Bookshop for the timely provision of reference material.

ISBN: 978 1 4728 1549 1
PDF ISBN: 978 1 4728 1550 7
ePub ISBN: 978 1 4728 1551 4

Index by Sandra Shotter
Typeset in Adobe Garamond and Gill Sans
Originated by PDQ Media, Bungay, UK
Printed in China through World Print Ltd.

16 17 18 19 20   10 9 8 7 6 5 4 3 2 1

Osprey Publishing supports the Woodland Trust, the UK's leading woodland
conservation charity. Between 2014 and 2018 our donations will be spent
on their Centenary Woods project in the UK.

www.ospreypublishing.com

CONTENTS

FOREWORD

'There is a Spitfire so go out there and fly it, and if you break it, there will be hell to pay.'

Thus spoke the voice of authority.

A week previously and direct from training, I had been posted to a Spitfire squadron stationed at Northolt. With only 146 hours total flying, of which 95 were solo, and never having ever seen a Spitfire, let alone flown one, I was of little use to them because the following morning, after joining,

they were on operations over Dunkirk. So a week later, at Duxford, where the squadron had gone to regroup and refit, I found myself walking out to fly a Spitfire for the very first time.

In view of my lack of flying experience I must confess to a degree of apprehension as I approached this lithe creature, a Spitfire, single-seat interceptor fighter. She looked absolutely right waiting there, elegant, delicate and relaxed, a graceful and utterly

Spitfire VB R6923 was amongst the many aircraft flown by Geoffrey Wellum during his 15-month tour with No 92 Squadron. Originally built as a Mk IB and delivered to No 19 Squadron in July 1940, the fighter was relegated to No 7 OTU when persistent jamming with the aeroplane's 20 mm cannon saw all Mk IBs swapped by No 19 Squadron for standard Spitfire IIAs. Converted into a Spitfire VB in April 1941, issued to No 92 Squadron, this aircraft was shot down by Bf 109s (possibly from JG 26) over the Channel on 21 June 1941 and during 'Circus 16', its pilot, Sergeant G. W. Ashton, bailing out and being rescued. (via Phil Jarrett)

beautiful aeroplane. The cockpit, although somewhat confined, had a friendly atmosphere about it. Sitting there, as I looked out over the curved wing, a feeling of unreality came over me. What a privilege to be here in this situation. How many pilots in the Royal Air Force would give their right arms to be here in my place?

Due to the narrow undercarriage, on taxiing, I found the Spitfire to be less stable than most aircraft, and because of the long nose, the view forward was restricted to say the least. But on the ground is not where this lovely aeroplane is meant to be. Her natural element was in the air, and once there she was a thing transformed. She seemed to just slip through the air and flow about the sky responding eagerly and lightly to every demand made of her by control input – I felt part and parcel with the Spitfire. We were as one. From that moment began forever a lasting love affair with this remarkable aircraft, and as I gained experience so my affection, if anything, grew.

There followed those momentous days of September 1940, in what is now known as the Battle of Britain. I felt a confidence and trust with my Spitfire. We were partners. She accepted with understanding every abuse I inflicted upon her to such an extent that I felt confident that if I could see my antagonist in his Me 109, I could always out fly him in a Spitfire. It was always the enemy you did not see who shot you down.

For the fighter sweeps and bomber escorts of 1941 and 1942 we flew the Spitfire Mk VB armed with cannon and an upgraded Merlin engine, the Merlin 45. These improvements did nothing to dispel the aircraft's superb handling qualities, nor for that matter in the latter marks of Spitfire, the Mks VIII, XI and XVI with the Merlin 60 series engines.

Throughout those early desperate years of World War 2 the Spitfire never ever let me down. In spite of being shot up on occasions she always brought me safely home both in the Battle of Britain and in what seemed the long stretch back across the Channel from Northern France and Belgium – and the Channel could look very uninviting at times!

As a young man you cannot go to war in a Spitfire and expect to forget about it. The experience stays with you in detail forever and the love for the Spitfire remains with you deeply for the whole of your life.

There are very few of the public at large who are not acquainted with the name Spitfire, and to those and devotees of this magnificent design concept, I most strongly commend this painstakingly researched book, which contains detailed photographs of the very highest quality taken by John Dibbs. John is a world renowned photographer who is known for his excellence in photographing military aircraft. This book is therefore a must for all those who have a love and admiration for the Spitfire.

Squadron Leader Geoffrey Wellum DFC
November 2015

No 92 Squadron flight commander Flight Lieutenant Brian Kingcome and his wingman, Flying Officer Geoffrey Wellum, who was known as 'Boy' throughout the unit. Wellum rated Kingcome, who was an ace, as 'the best leader I ever flew with'. This photograph was taken in June 1941. (via John Dibbs)

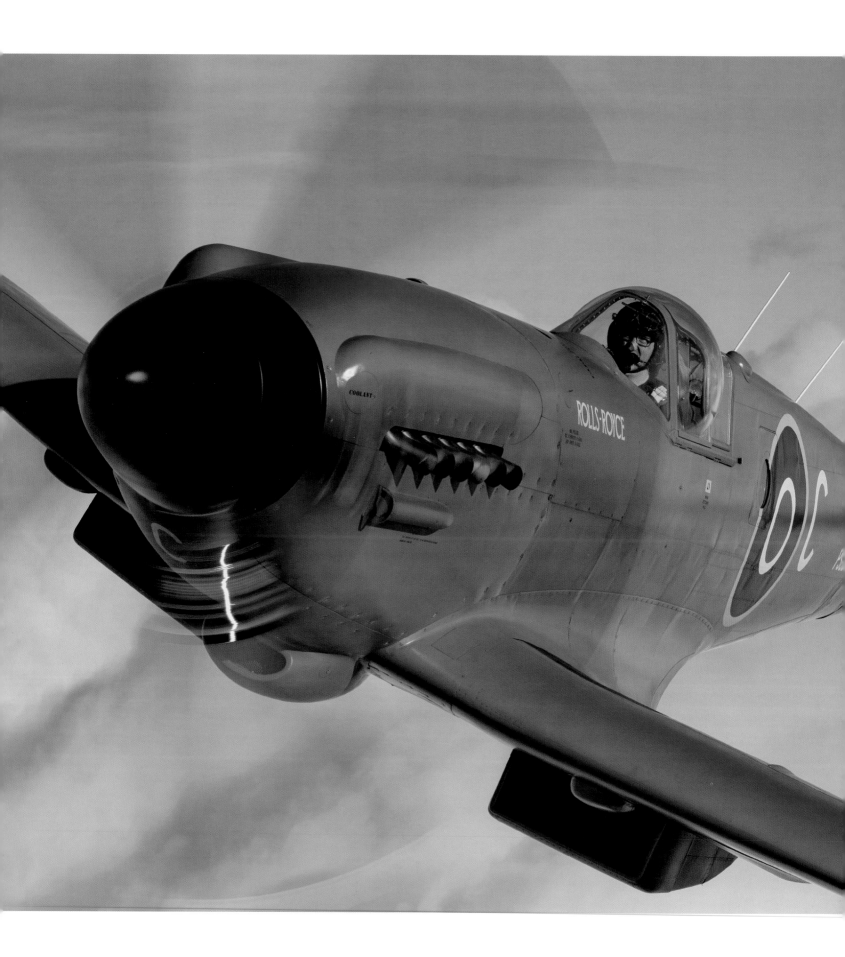

INTRODUCTION

11

Rolls-Royce plc Chief Test Pilot Phill O'Dell at the controls of Spitfire PR XIX.

My earliest memories of the Spitfire are disappointingly a little vague and distant. I know I ham-fistedly muddled my way through building a Mk IX model, but sadly I remember little else. The first clear recollection of my more recent association with the aircraft came on a miserable winter's night when I walked through the doors of Rolls-Royce's Heritage Flight hangar, then at Filton near Bristol. Returning from a test flight at Warton, I had just heard that I had been supremely lucky and was to become the Chief Test Pilot of Rolls-Royce. During the previous few weeks, whilst awaiting news of the outcome of the application process, I hadn't allowed myself to think about, look at, or let alone touch a Spitfire – the thought of actually flying one had still been very much an unlikely dream. Suddenly, on hearing that I had been successful, it had all become an exciting (but a little bit terrifying!) reality. Sitting in the aircraft that night, with an eerie wind buffeting the old World War 2 hangar, the prospect was slowly sinking in.

Over the next few months I began my preparations to fly the Rolls-Royce Spitfire PR XIX for the first time. Having luckily been flying a variety of tail-wheeled aircraft for many years leading up to this point, the basics should at least be 'squared away', or would they? My next flight in a tail-wheeled aircraft was probably one of my worst. I was utterly overwhelmed with the new challenge, and knowledge that I would soon be flying an icon of world aviation, probably the most recognisable aircraft anywhere on the planet and a priceless, much loved, symbol of freedom, fortitude and toil. I am proud to say Rolls-Royce has maintained 'PS' as a tribute to those that gave their lives, or simply 'worked till they dropped' many years ago, but on this day that knowledge was getting in the way of successful

Rolls-Royce plc Chief Test Pilot Phill O'Dell. (Rolls-Royce plc)

'3-point' landings! I persevered, and shortly afterwards flew the Harvard for a number of trips, mostly from the rear seat, as a preparation for sitting behind a huge '12-cylinder blindfold' – the Griffon engine!

I've often wondered what may have been lost or gained by flying the Griffon before the Merlin. It is inevitable that in my role within an engine manufacturing company I'll naturally be interested and somewhat focused on the powerplant of any aircraft I fly. Since my first flight in the Spitfire behind a Griffon, I've been even luckier and further privileged to go on and fly many different marks of the aircraft, and, of course, the 'Merlin'. My first trip behind a Merlin was in a newly restored Spitfire IX flying from a small airfield in Brazil,

not far from São Paolo. To be very honest, I was slightly distracted at the time, mostly by my struggle to navigate across the unfamiliar terrain of Brazil. It was not until some months later, back in the UK and flying on relatively stress-free transits, that I was able to much better appreciate the differences between the two fabulous engines. The Griffon is undoubtedly more brutal. The engine note is different in pitch (and noticeable to the experienced ear) and the levels of vibration greater and different in frequency. The Merlin is smoother and perhaps a little 'more civilised' in comparison. However, this could, unfairly, give a false impression, as the Merlin remains phenomenally powerful. Both the Merlin and the Griffon are remarkable engines. Each produces a sound shocking in its strength and power, but delightful in the richness and detail of its tone. Either could quite simply be the most wonderful sound in aviation.

A great delight and absolute honour of my role is to meet many veterans and have the immense privilege to discuss a whole range of topics relating to the Spitfire. It is clear how much they all appreciated the importance, the lifeblood, provided by the engine, but equally everyone talks of 'wearing' the aircraft itself. Interestingly, it is not just the pilots that talk about this feeling, it is often their families and friends. The genuine gratitude amongst them all for how the Spitfire kept them safe is so noticeable and obvious. It is this fact that probably leads to the belief that the aircraft is actually 'alive', its soul being apparent to anyone lucky enough to fly in the aircraft, whether occupying the front seat or flying in 'the back' of the growing number of two-seat examples. Each individual aircraft, not just the different marks, has a character – quirks of engineering perhaps, or a product of their history, provenance or upbringing. Who knows, but they are certainly all 'alive'.

This soul is linked to the fascinating and remarkable people that surround the aircraft. I have written this introduction just two days after being fortunate enough to have spent a fascinating evening in the company of Geoffrey Wellum. It would be wrong to eulogise the aircraft without mentioning the remarkable men and women that accompanied it. Geoffrey is the most perfect example. His book, *First Light*, and the subsequent time he has devoted to telling the story of his life, has changed the impressions and understanding of many people. Through his remarkably candid, lively, honest and wonderfully descriptive writing he has helped us understand the terrors, the pressures, the fears and the highlights of a remarkable part of our history. His love and warmth for the Spitfire puts so much into context.

It is absolutely fitting that Geoffrey has written the foreword to this marvelous book. It is also fitting that through their exhaustive, detailed and excellent work both John and Tony have provided us with further illuminating and wonderful knowledge and images of surely the world's greatest aircraft. Many excellent books have been published about the Spitfire, but for me, this volume truly captures the emotion, spirit, raw energy and passion of the aircraft. Both in words and pictures we see how the Spitfire grew from the early marks through to the significantly changed and enhanced final variants. Throughout the book, their second in a series detailing the life of the 'Spit', John and Tony repeatedly capture the romance and aura that surrounds the aircraft, supported with numerous interesting facts about its growth and development.

From that first day I sat in a Spitfire on that stormy winter's evening, I have grown to appreciate, trust and adore the aircraft. This book brings all those emotions together in a superb journey through the life of a most treasured icon.

Phill O'Dell
Chief Test Pilot
Rolls-Royce plc
November 2015

The Spitfire has been pretty much omnipresent in my life for as long as I can remember. I find it as defining as the Union Jack when it comes to Great Britain.

If you strip away the modern concept of the warbird, then it is truly amazing and would likely have been deemed impossible in 1936 or 1940 to think that in 2016, 80 years on from its first flight, there would not only be one Spitfire still flying but that its popularity and the population of flying aircraft is burgeoning.

I have been most fortunate to have found a career that allows me to be around the most beautiful aircraft ever to fly. It is without doubt my favourite aeroplane to shoot. You don't have to look for a good angle. The fact that there is barely a straight line on this aircraft was probably an engineer's nightmare, but a delight for anyone else, especially a photographer, to look upon, and the angles find you. Sat atop the English countryside with a Mk I or Mk V off your wing is not something you just witness, you feel it. Man-made perfection, and it's called a Spitfire.

Since the first volume of *Spitfire – Flying Legend* was published in 1996, such is the draw of this machine that Tony Holmes and I have been able to assemble another volume with nearly all new machines to fill each chapter. We hope this book will act as a tribute to the men and women that helped create, build and fly this iconic aircraft, whose actions, deeds and sacrifice created a rare kind of immortality.

We owe a debt of thanks to those before us and each one of us now can help carry it forward.

John Dibbs
December 2015

CHAPTER ONE

THE EARLY MARKS

SPITFIRE F IA N3200

Presently the oldest airworthy Spitfire in the world, F IA N3200 was built during 1939 as part of an order for 200 fighters received by Supermarine from the Air Ministry in September 1938. Following its first flight from Eastleigh airport, in Hampshire, on 29 November 1939, the fighter was sent to No 8 Maintenance Unit (MU) at Little Rissington, in Gloucestershire, three days later and stored until issued to No 19 Squadron at Duxford, in Cambridgeshire, on 19 April 1940. It is possible that N3200 served as an attrition replacement for K9858, which had crashed on take-off from Horsham St Faith, in Norfolk, after its pilot, Flying Officer Douglas Bader, omitted to select the correct propeller pitch setting and the fighter cartwheeled across a ploughed field when it ran out of runway.

Although N3200 had the unit's 'QV' code letters applied to its fuselage shortly after its arrival at the Cambridgeshire fighter station, no individual aircraft identification letter was ever added – an odd omission for the period.

Pilots would usually fly whatever aircraft was serviceable at the time, and this was indeed the case with N3200 during its short time with No 19 Squadron. Amongst those individuals to routinely take the fighter aloft was the unit's CO, Squadron Leader Geoffrey Stephenson. Like N3200, he had only recently joined No 19 Squadron after its previous commanding officer, Squadron Leader Henry Cozens, had been promoted and posted to a staff position. A pre-war fighter pilot, Stephenson had also previously served as a Qualified Flying Instructor at the RAF's Central Flying School (CFS) at Upavon, in Wiltshire.

On 25 May N3200 was amongst the 12 Spitfires flown from Duxford to Hornchurch, in Essex, when No 19 Squadron was temporarily posted south to support the British Expeditionary

Light and agile, the F IA was a real favourite amongst experienced Spitfire pilots thanks to the responsiveness of its controls – as dramatically demonstrated here in the skies over Cambridgeshire.

Force as it fell back in the direction of Dunkirk in the face of the German *Blitzkrieg*. Amongst the pilots sent to Hornchurch was Pilot Officer Michael Lyne:

We had been sent south to take the place of squadrons shot to pieces in the early stages of the battle of Dunkirk. To us, the mess at Hornchurch had a new atmosphere, with people clearing the rooms of kit belonging to casualties and the Station Commander insisting on closing the bar and sending us to bed to be ready for the battles that awaited us.

On 26 May we were called on to patrol over the beaches. I will always remember heading off to the east and seeing the columns of smoke from the Dunkirk oil storage tanks. We patrolled for some time without seeing any aircraft and received no information from the British radar, then called RDF [Radio Direction Finders]. We had received excellent VHF [Very High Frequency] radios shortly before, but they were only of use between ourselves on that patrol. Suddenly we saw ahead, going towards Calais where the Rifle Brigade was holding out, about 40

German aircraft – we were 12. Geoffrey Stephenson [flying N3200] aligned us for attack in sections of three on a formation of Ju 87s. As a former CFS A1 instructor, he was a precise flier and obedient to the book [RAF Manual of Air Tactics, issued in 1938], which stipulated an overtaking speed of 30 mph. What the book never foresaw was that we would attack Ju 87s doing just about 130 mph. The CO led his section (Pilot Officer P. V. 'Watty' Watson as his No 2 and me as his No 3) straight up behind the Ju 87s, which looked very relaxed – they thought we were their fighter escort. Their leader had been very clever and had pulled his formation away towards England, so that when they turned in towards Calais he would protect their rear. Alas for him we were coming, by sheer chance, from Dunkirk rather than from Ramsgate.

Meanwhile, Stephenson realised that we were closing far too fast. I remember his call 'No 19 Squadron! Prepare to attack', then to us 'Red Section, throttling back, throttling back, throttling back'.

We were virtually formatting on the last section of Ju 87s, at an incredibly dangerous speed in the presence of enemy fighters – and behind us the rest

Spitfire F IA N3200 became something of an attraction for German troops on the beach at Sangatte, as this photograph discovered in August 2010 clearly shows. Squadron Leader Gordon Stephenson had made a textbook wheels-up landing in the fighter on 28 May 1940 after its engine had been hit by return fire from Ju 87s. He clearly got some rounds off too prior to his forced landing, as the fabric covering over the fighter's gun ports has been shot away. (via Peter R. Arnold)

of the squadron were staggering along at a similar speed. Of course the Ju 87s could not imagine that we were a threat. Then Stephenson told us to take a target each and fire. As far as I know we got the last three – we could hardly have done otherwise – then we broke away and saw nothing of the work of the rest of the squadron, but it must have been dodgy for the last section as the Ju 87s' Me 109 escorts had by then started to come around behind us. As I was looking round for friends after the break I came under fire from the rear for the first time – and did not at first know it. The first signs were mysterious little corkscrews of smoke passing my starboard wing. Then I heard a slow 'thump, thump', and realised that I was being attacked by a Me 109 firing machine guns with tracer and cannon banging away. I broke away sharpish and lost him.

I made a wide sweep and came back to the Calais area to find about five Ju 87s going round in a tight defensive circle. The German fighters had disappeared, so I flew at the circle in order to attack the aircraft from head-on, giving it a long squirt. It must have been at this stage that I was hit by return fire, for when I got back to Hornchurch I found

The fighter did not remain intact for long, however, with its engine cowlings, gun covers, part of the rudder and tail wheel all 'souveniered' by German soldiers. It also appears that some of them had taken potshots at the fuselage. (via Peter R. Arnold)

Squadron Leader Geoffrey Stephenson (seen here post-war as an air commodore) spent more than five years in captivity after being shot down during his very first action, in N3200. A pre-war aviator rated as one of the most capable fighter pilots in the RAF, he remained in the service upon returning to Britain in 1945. Following a posting as Aide-de-Camp to King George VI, Stephenson was given command of the Central Fighter Establishment. It was whilst serving in this role that he was killed in a flying accident in an F-100A Super Sabre on 8 November 1954 during an exchange tour with the US Air Force at Eglin Air Force Base, in Florida. (via Sarah Joyce)

bullet holes in the wing, the rounds having punctured a tyre.

Alas my friend Watson was never seen again, and Stephenson made a forced landing in France and was eventually taken prisoner.

Upon his return to Hornchurch Lyne confirmed with No 19 Squadron's Intelligence Officer that he had seen Stephenson down a Ju 87. Squadronmate Sergeant Jack Potter, flying in another section, stated that he then spotted the CO's Spitfire in an apparently 'controlled glide over the French coast,

RIGHT N3200 and fellow Calais beach wreck Spitfire IA P9374 fly in close formation from Duxford during the summer of 2015. The latter machine, of No 92 Squadron, had been shot down 48 hours prior to N3200 and was recovered in 1980. Both owned by Mark One Partners when this photograph was taken, these aeroplanes are presently the oldest flying examples of the Spitfire in the world.

The wreckage of N3200 emerges from the sand at Sangatte during the spring of 1986, the aircraft appearing to be remarkably intact despite being buried for 46 years. (via Peter R. Arnold)

leaving a thin trail of blue smoke behind it'. N3200 had had its radiator holed almost certainly by a round fired by a gunner in a Ju 87. The fighter's Merlin III engine quickly overheated and seized, leaving Stephenson with little option but to force land on the beach at Sangatte, west of Calais. He abandoned his virtually intact fighter on the beach. 'No German soldiers immediately rushed out, so I began to think of rejoining English or French troops besieged in Calais or Boulogne', Stephenson recorded in his diary. He then attempted to return to England during an 11-day ordeal that saw him cross 100 miles of occupied France and Belgium until he reached the US Embassy in Brussels. Hoping to enlist help in securing his escape, Stephenson was declined assistance due to America's neutrality and captured shortly thereafter.

While its pilot commenced almost five years of incarceration in various Prisoner of War camps (including Colditz), N3200 was initially an object of some curiosity for German soldiers newly billeted in the area. However, it soon sank into the tidal sand and was forgotten about until unusually strong currents revealed the remains of the fighter 45 years later.

During the spring of 1986 the wreckage was excavated and placed on display in the museum at the La Forteresse de Mimoyecques for a number of years. In November 2000 it was acquired (along with fellow Calais beach wreck Spitfire IA P9374 of No 92 Squadron, which had been shot down 48 hours before N3200 and recovered in 1980) by Simon Marsh and Thomas Kaplan of Mark One Partners and collected from the museum by a team

from Airframe Assemblies Ltd of Sandown, on the Isle of Wight. Here, the fuselage was reconstructed using period blueprints. N3200 was transferred to the Colchester workshop of warbird restorer Craig Charleston in March 2002 and then onward to Historic Flying Ltd (HFL) at Duxford in September 2007. With the reconstructed fuselage being taken out of the jig at Airframe Assemblies Ltd on September 2010, the restoration of N3200 soon began to make great progress as the airframe followed P9374 through HFL's Duxford workshop.

Briefed by Mark One Partners to make the aircraft as original as possible, HFL ensured that the fighter was fitted with the correct equipment for the period. Fabric-covered ailerons, stainless steel screws and ammunition chutes unique to the Spitfire I were just some of the myriad 'period' features included in the restoration by HFL's engineers. N3200 also had eight Browning 0.303-in machine guns and ammunition belts (the latter dated 1940) in their boxes installed in the wings. Finally, the fighter's rare Merlin III was overhauled by Retro Track and Air in Cam, Gloucestershire, the engine being paired with a correct two-position de Havilland bracket-type propeller unit.

N3200 completed its first post-restoration flight on 26 March 2014 from Duxford with HFL Managing Director and Chief Pilot John Romain at the controls. On 9 July 2015, in a ceremony attended by the Duke of Cambridge, N3200 was donated to the Imperial War Museum at Duxford by Thomas Kaplan.

OPPOSITE HFL was instructed by Mark One Partners to restore N3200 to its original condition, and the company's engineers worked hard to fulfil this brief during the fighter's six-and-a-half-year restoration at Duxford. The cockpit is perhaps the ultimate example of their craftsmanship. Note the missing instrument to the left of the GM 2 gunsight, its absence being explained by HFL detail fitter Mark Parr: 'A classic case of getting things right is what we did with the flap gauge. On Spitfires, the flaps are either deployed or not – there are no in between settings, but on the very earliest ones there was a little gauge inside the cockpit indicating up and down. It was a concept that they soon deleted as the pilot only had to look out the window to check the position of the flaps. If you look in the cockpit of both of our Mk Is there is a hole where the flap gauge would have been. We manufactured the gauges, but after speaking with various people who have done a lot of Spitfire-related archaeological digs, we realised that the instrument would not have actually been present on our aircraft. They've have been removed, leaving a space, and eventually that space would have doubtless been used for something else.'

TOP According to the Air Ministry pattern guide for small fighters published in Air Publication 970, the instructions to manufacturers and RAF units alike for the application of aircraft serial numbers was that they should be painted 'underneath the lower planes and at the rear end of the fuselage'. This order was open to interpretation by Fighter Command units in the build-up to World War 2, with some aircraft appearing with underwing serial numbers, or none at all! However, any ambiguity was removed with the issuing of Air Ministry Order A154 in November 1939, which stated that all serial numbers were to be painted on the sides of the rear fuselage only, cancelling any previous instructions. No 19 Squadron at Duxford, however, ensured that all of its Spitfire IAs had correctly sized serial numbers in the appropriate location by late 1939.

ABOVE N3200 was adorned with standard 35-inch Type A roundels, which had been applied prior to the fighter being issued to No 19 Squadron in April 1940. On 1 May word was received at Duxford, in the form of Air Ministry signal X485, that all RAF Commands were to immediately modify the fuselage roundels on their aircraft, encircling them with a ring of yellow. The latter was to be the same width as the blue ring, thus producing a 49-inch roundel on many Hurricanes and Spitfires – including N3200. This change was the result of increased combat experience, particularly in France and Norway, which had shown that the existing national markings were insufficiently visible in the heat of battle. The fighter's non-standard rearview mirror was an MG-type item that had been privately sourced by a pilot (possibly the CO) serving on the squadron and fitted by his rigger.

OPPOSITE The standard factory finish (Aluminium, Night and White) for the under-surfaces of Spitfires built between 24 April 1939 and 11 June 1940 has been faithfully applied to N3200 by HFL, as have all the groundcrew handling stencils.

One aspect of N3200's unit markings was most definitely non-standard – it lacked an aircraft identification code letter aft of the roundel. Like all other Spitfires assigned to No 19 Squadron in the spring of 1940, however, the aeroplane bore the approximately 36-inch high grey 'QV' code assigned to the unit in September 1939 in place of the 'WZ' code that it had used from October of the previous year. Aside from the squadron code, N3200 also had its fin stripes applied at Duxford after its arrival in the frontline. The Air Ministry issued an amendment on 16 May 1940 stating that all new production Spitfires were to have such stripes, consisting of three seven-inch bands. This marking was retrospectively applied at squadron-level to aeroplanes already in operational service.

OPPOSITE TOP N3200 emerged from the Supermarine works in Southampton in the A-scheme Dark Green and Dark Earth camouflage pattern applied to all Spitfires with a serial ending in an even number.

OPPOSITE BOTTOM From head on, the Spitfire F IA's modest radiator can be seen beneath the starboard wing. This worked effectively once the fighter was in the air, but it proved barely up to the job of keeping the engine from boiling over when the fighter was on the ground prior to take-off. Indeed, the Merlin could overheat in as little as four or five minutes on warm summer days as the undercarriage, when extended, partly blocked the radiator. Furthermore, when the flaps were down this also blanked the rear of the radiator off, further restricting airflow.

LEFT With its left aileron in the 'up' position, N3200 commences a gentle roll for the benefit of the camera.

SPITFIRE F IA X4650

Built by Supermarine in Southampton, X4650 was part of the third order for 500 Spitfires placed with the manufacturer by the Air Ministry on 9 June 1940. Flown for the first time at Eastleigh on 23 October that same year, the fighter was delivered to No 24 MU at Ternhill, in Shropshire, two days later. Following preparation for operational use, X4650 was supplied to No 54 Squadron at Catterick on 14 November 1940.

One of Fighter Command's leading units during the Battle of Britain, No 54 Squadron had achieved 54.5 aerial victories during 19 days of combat flying from Hornchurch, but it had lost 20 aircraft in the process. Sent to Catterick, in No 13 Group, on 3 September for a rest from frontline operations in No 11 Group, the unit had been re-designated a 'C' Class squadron by Fighter Command. This meant that it could be stripped of most of its operational pilots, who would be sent to 'A' Class units in Nos 10, 11 and 12 Groups. In their place, new pilots would be posted in fresh from Operational Training Units (OTUs). For the five original pilots that remained with No 54 Squadron following its re-designation, their energies would now be devoted to the training of these neophyte aviators.

One of the makeshift instructors was decorated Battle of Britain ace Flight Lieutenant Al Deere, who, along with fellow ace and flight commander Flight Lieutenant George Gribble, devised a training syllabus for No 54 Squadron. 'We concentrated on cine-gun exercises', Deere explained in his autobiography, *Nine Lives*:

...and only included formation flying as a means of judging a pilot's confidence and ability to fly in cloud in formation and to carry out fast climbs to height. From the moment the pilot got into his aircraft he was made conscious of the fact that his primary aim was to bring his sights to bear on the enemy. No matter what the exercise, we invariably finished up with the pilots in line astern formation, at about 200-yard intervals, and briefed that not only must they follow the leader, but that they must

endeavour to keep taking cine-gun shots while so doing. In this way we hoped they would soon get out of the inbred training habit of flying their aircraft always in relation to the horizon and with constant reference to instruments, rather than by feel and instinct. We wanted them to be able to get their sights on a target and to keep them there without worrying about the attitude of their own aircraft in relation to the horizon or the ground. The principle must be that the aircraft is but the agent to carry the guns, and the latter must be brought to bear whatever the antics of the target.

It was amazing how quickly the cine-camera results, and the flying, improved. Furthermore, it was soon apparent which of the new arrivals were going to make really good fighter pilots. It was up to the squadron to say when a particular pilot was ready to go south, and the doubtful ones were kept back as long as possible. A pilot was certified as fully operational only after he had passed the most stringent tests, the final one of which was a dogfight with his flight commander or his deputy. During the course of one these final tests, I had a remarkable escape.

A particularly promising pilot by the name of Sergeant Howard Squire [flying Spitfire IA X4650] was keen for me to take him on his final test, and I agreed. [On 28 December 1940] We climbed to 10,000 ft and I told him to position himself astern and

ABOVE LEFT Sergeant Howard Squire was at the controls of Spitfire F IA X4650 when he accidentally chopped off the tail of the Spitfire flown by his flight leader, Battle of Britain ace Flight Lieutenant Al Deere, resulting in both pilots having to take to their parachutes. (via John Dibbs)

ABOVE New Zealander Flight Lieutenant Al Deere is introduced to a packed audience at the HMV factory in Hayes, Middlesex, in August 1941. The company made radios for Spitfires and other RAF aircraft throughout World War 2. (via John Dibbs)

OPPOSITE Sergeant Howard Squire's logbook reveals just how much flying he had done in the lead-up to his collision with Flight Lieutenant Deere on 28 December 1940. Unlike the veteran Kiwi pilot he hit, Squire was back in the air the very next day. Clearly December was an eventful month for the fighter pilot as he had crashed on take-off exactly three weeks earlier!

No 54 SQUADRON. CATTERICK.

YEAR 1940		AIRCRAFT		PILOT, OR 1ST PILOT	2ND PILOT, PUPIL OR PASSENGER	DUTY (INCLUDING RESULTS AND REMARKS)	SINGLE-ENGINE AIRCRAFT				MULTI-ENGINE		
MONTH	DATE	Type	No.				DAY DUAL (1)	DAY PILOT (2)	NIGHT DUAL (3)	NIGHT PILOT (4)	DAY DUAL (5)	DAY 1ST PILOT (6)	2ND PILOT (7)
		—	—	—	—	TOTALS BROUGHT FORWARD							
						LOCAL FLYING							
DEC	4	SPITFIRE	K.	SELF	—	FORMATION.							
DEC	5	SPITFIRE	K.	SELF	—	FORMATION No 2.	64.50	92.35					
DEC	5	SPITFIRE	C	SELF	—	FORMATION No 3.		.40					
DEC	7	SPITFIRE	I	SELF	—	CRASHED ON TAKE-OFF		.45					
DEC	7	SPITFIRE	I	SELF	—	AEROBATICS. ROLLS. STALLS		.40					
DEC	8	SPITFIRE	K	SELF	—	FORMATION No 3		.40					
DEC	8	SPITFIRE	K	SELF	—	AIR FIGHTING & AEROBATICS		—					
DEC	17	SPITFIRE	F.	SELF	—	AIR FIGHTING		.55					
DEC	19	SPITFIRE	J	SELF	—	FORMATION. 2 & 3		.25					
DEC	19	SPITFIRE	G	SELF	—	FORMATION. 3.		.55					
DEC	19	SPITFIRE	G	SELF	—	FORMATION. 3.		1.00					
DEC	19	SPITFIRE	G.	SELF	—	FORMATION		.35					
DEC	20	SPITFIRE	G	SELF	—	FORMATION		.35					
DEC	20	SPITFIRE	F	SELF	—	AIR FIGHTING & AEROBATICS		.35					
DEC	20	SPITFIRE	J	SELF	—	PATROL		.15					
DEC	20	SPITFIRE	F	SELF	—	PRACTICE BATTLE CLIMB		.35					
DEC	21	SPITFIRE	C	SELF	—	PATROL		1.00					
DEC	21	SPITFIRE	A	SELF	—	FORMATION.		.40			.30		
DEC	22	SPITFIRE	J	SELF	—	FORMATION		.35					
DEC	22	SPITFIRE	D	SELF	—	PATROL		1.00					
DEC	23	SPITFIRE	E	SELF	—	SQUADRON FORMATION.		.35					
DEC	27	SPITFIRE	C X4650	SELF	—	DOG FIGHTING.		.35					
DEC	28	SPITFIRE	A	SELF	—	FORMATION No 3.		1.45					
DEC	29	SPITFIRE	L	SELF	—			.25					
								.35					
								.35					
						GRAND TOTAL [Cols. (1) to (10)] 173 Hrs 45 Mins.							
						TOTALS CARRIED FORWARD	64.50	100.55			.30		

LEFT The restored fuselage and tail assembly of X4650 sits on trestles in the Biggin Hill Heritage Hangar shortly after its arrival from The Aircraft Restoration Company's Duxford facility in June 2011.

CENTRE A close-up of the starboard elevator and unconnected elevator tab, both of which contain much of their original structure – with approved repairs carried out where necessary. Like the fighter's rudder, which is an original early type as fitted to the Mk I, the elevators were re-covered with Irish linen.

BOTTOM During the restoration of X4650, wherever possible, engineers faithfully followed the original rivet holes during the assembly of the airframe. Although hard to see once the aeroplane was painted, some of the lines of rivets were quite uneven, proving that speed and functionality took precedence over neatness in Supermarine's Eastleigh factory during the early war years.

RIGHT Correct three-stack exhaust manifolds protrude through X4650's engine cowlings.

BELOW RIGHT Although Peter Monk of the Biggin Hill Heritage Hangar acquired a Merlin III engine and Mk I propeller during 15-plus years of collecting original components for the rebuilding of X4650, the decision was taken early on in the project to install a longer-life, highly reliable, Merlin 35 instead. While externally almost identical to the earlier Merlin III, the later engine's overhaul time and general strength were plusses that could not be ignored in such a rare airworthy machine.

below at about 250 yards, using the range-bar on his reflector to get his distance. A dogfight now ensued, with me doing everything I knew to get him off my tail until, as usually happens in aerial combat, I found myself down to about 3,000 ft, which was well below the safety height we had set for this exercise.

'Okay "Red Two", I'll climb up again to 10,000 ft and we'll have another go. You are doing fine, but please keep your distance at about 250 yards – you are getting far too close'.

Squire acknowledged this message and dropped back to the required distance. When at the desired height, I again started throwing the aircraft about, determined this time to get him off my tail. It is most difficult, and indeed almost impossible, with the rear vision afforded from the cockpit of a Spitfire, to keep an aircraft behind and below in sight for every second of a dogfight. After a series of hectic manoeuvres culminating in a steep turn, I could not see Squire, and in order to check if I had

ABOVE Every component in the cockpit of X4650 is authentic, and if it is not from the original aircraft it has been sourced from another Spitfire I recovered or obtained from 1940 surplus stock. Dominating this view are the Barr and Stroud GM 2 reflector gunsight and the 1940-stamped control column. The latter is topped by a spade grip complete with a worn red anodised firing button. Genuine Spitfire I spade grips are almost impossible to find, with reproduction or Hurricane grips often being used in restorations. The grip in X4650, however, is an ultra-scarce pre-1939 example that is so early in the Spitfire's production life that it is stamped 'Dunlop Patent Applied For'. This particular spade grip saw action in the Battle of Britain, and was recovered from a downed Spitfire in the summer of 1940 by an RAF salvage crew. The GM 2 is also a very early, rare, reflector sight with the oval sighting glass – the correct type for a Mk I.

been successful in shaking him off I reversed my turn quickly. For a split second I caught a glimpse of the nose of his aircraft right on top of me and the next second he had flown into me. His propeller chewed clean through my tailplane and immediately my Spitfire [X4276] whipped into a vicious spin, completely out of control.

In a matter of seconds I had jettisoned the hood and proceeded with the business of bailing out, having, of course, first carried out the necessary preliminaries of releasing my cockpit straps and freeing my R/T [radio transmitter] lead. To get out of the aircraft was not going to be easy, as I soon discovered. I was spinning at an unnaturally fast rate, and descending at a very high speed. Try as I might, I couldn't overcome the centrifugal forces that kept me anchored to my seat, and no amount of pulling with my hands on the side of the cockpit would overcome it. Again and again I tried until quite unexpectedly I floated out of the cockpit. I can only think that at some stage of the spin the centrifugal force was less, and I had chosen then to exert a little more strength. Anyhow, I was free, but only for a second or two. I was blown on to the remnants of the shattered tail unit, where I stuck fast. I twisted and turned, kicked and fought with every ounce of my strength until finally I broke free.

Instinctively I reached for the parachute rip-cord handle, and it was then that I realised that my parachute had been partially torn from my back. The handle was not in its usual place and the whole parachute pack was whirling around my head as I tumbled over and over, the ground uncomfortably close. I can distinctly remember saying to myself at this juncture, 'Fancy being killed this way', meaning, of course, not in combat.

When all seemed lost my parachute miraculously opened of its own accord – partially as it turned out – and only just in time, for I seemed to hit the ground at the same moment. I was horizontal when I struck, and this position, coupled with the fact that I ended up in a farmer's cesspool, which cushioned the impact, probably saved my life. I very nearly drowned in the foul stuff (but, in the circumstances, perhaps sweet!), as with a badly injured back making it agony to move, I had the

greatest difficulty in crawling free. A passing motorist came to my assistance, and together with his wife, helped me into his car and was good enough to drive me back to Catterick, some seven miles away.

Sergeant Howard Squire gave an account of the incident in a letter he wrote in April 1988:

On 28 December I took off with Flight Lieutenant Deere for the second time for air-fighting practice. It was a cold winter day, sunny with little or no cloud. We climbed to 10,000 ft over the aerobatics area northeast of Catterick. I was instructed to start the exercise by trying to hang on to his tail while he took evasive action, with the object of throwing me off. After a strenuous bout, during which I hung on and was very pleased with my efforts, I suddenly found I was closing very rapidly. I have always believed that he turned up-sun and slowed to check I was still with him, climbing slightly. To avoid him I closed the throttle and pushed the stick forward to dive under him. There was a resounding crash as I caught his tail, passing under him.

He vanished and I found myself with a vibrating engine still in balanced flight, but with no hood and the rear fuselage and part of the fin flattened – I assume from both the initial impact and his prop. I decided the damage was such that I might not be able to get back, and that I would best get out. I undid my Sutton harness, stood up on the seat and, as the aircraft was still stable, stood on the flattened rear of the cockpit and dived clear. I knew I was high, so I delayed opening my parachute until I had fallen well clear and had turned over a few times. When the ground came into view I pulled the ripcord. The aircraft I had been allocated had had someone else's parachute onboard – we must have taken off in a hurry. Anyway, it was not mine, and he was bigger than me. It opened with a bang and gave me a moment or two of acute discomfort until I could grasp the shroud lines and wriggle the leg straps into an easier position.

Like Al Deere, Squire landed safely and soon returned to flying. He was subsequently shot down

Meticulous research was undertaken by Peter Monk and his team in order to recreate the correct colours and finish of the standard RAF 'day scheme' worn by X4650 in service with No 54 Squadron. With its serial ending in an even number, the fighter would have had the A-scheme Dark Green and Dark Earth camouflage pattern applied at the factory in October 1940. Its fuselage was adorned with Type A1 35-inch roundels and the upper-surfaces of the wings featured standard 56-inch Type B two-colour roundels. The fighter's under-surfaces were finished in the pale blue-green shade officially known as Sky, which was adopted by the Air Ministry for all RAF fighters from 6 June 1940. For safety reasons, the Biggin Hill Heritage Hangar contracted Airframe Assemblies Ltd to construct the fighter's wings with new spars, although approximately one-third of X4650's original wing structure was incorporated into the restoration.

on his very first operational mission – still with No 54 Squadron – on 26 February 1941, falling victim to high-scoring Bf 109 ace Hauptmann Herbert Ihlefeld of I./LG 2.

Both Spitfires involved in the midair collision came down in rolling farmland east of the village of Kirkleavington, in North Yorkshire. Despite a relatively soft crash-landing near the banks of the River Leven, X4650 was deemed to have been damaged beyond repair by the RAF salvage crew sent to recover it. Following the removal of classified equipment the fighter was rolled into the river. With the eventual collapsing of the river bank, the Spitfire was hidden by water and clay for the best part of four decades.

However, during the hot summer of 1976, water levels in the Leven dropped to such an extent that the remains of X4650 were exposed. The aeroplane was recovered and then placed in storage for a further 19 years until acquired by warbird pilot and restorer Peter Monk. He had obtained numerous Spitfire I components from other crash sites, and he duly contracted Hull Aero Ltd of Bentwaters, in Suffolk, to reconstruct the fuselage of X4650. This was completed in October 2009, with the wings and tail unit being sourced from Airframe Assemblies Ltd. The fuselage was moved to Audley End, in Essex, that same month, before being transported to the Duxford premises of The Aircraft Restoration Company after being acquired by Comanche Warbirds, although the work had been contracted by Peter Monk. The aeroplane was moved again in June 2011 when X4650 was transferred to the Biggin Hill Heritage Hangar for systems fit, final assembly and test flying – this work was carried out by Peter Monk and his team of engineers. Finally, on 9 March 2012, Paul Bonhomme completed the fighter's first post-restoration flight. X4650 has been resident at Duxford ever since.

SPITFIRE F IIA P7350

Ordered as part of Contract No B981687/39 dated 12 April 1938, Spitfire F IIA P7350 was the fourteenth of 11,939 Spitfires built by the Castle Bromwich 'Shadow Factory' in Birmingham during World War 2. Test flown in early August 1940, the aeroplane was taken on charge by the RAF on the 13th of that same month and delivered to No 6 MU at Brize Norton, in Oxfordshire, four days later. P7350 was issued to No 266 Squadron at Wittering, in Cambridgeshire, on 6 September when the unit became one of the first in Fighter Command to receive Spitfire IIs in place of Mk Is – 18 Mk IIs were accepted by No 266 'Rhodesia' Squadron at Wittering on 5–6 September. Given the unit code 'UO-T', the aircraft moved with the unit to Martlesham Heath, in Norfolk, on 28 September and then on to Collyweston, in Northamptonshire, five days later. Part of No 12 Group, No 266 Squadron saw little action during P7350's time with the unit.

On 17 October the fighter was transferred to No 603 'City of Edinburgh' Squadron at Hornchurch, the ferry flight being undertaken by none other than Alex Henshaw, Chief Test Pilot at Castle Bromwich. The fighter was re-coded 'XT', although its individual aircraft code letter remains unknown. Eight days later the aeroplane was flown into action by 21-year-old Pole Pilot Officer Ludwik Martel, who had been transferred from No 54 Squadron to No 603 Squadron in early October. A cadet officer pilot in the Polish Air Force (PAF) when Germany

invaded on 1 September 1939, Martel had arrived in England, via Rumania and France, in early 1940. Commissioned into the RAF in May of that year, he had transferred to the reformed PAF three months later and joined No 54 Squadron at Hornchurch on 10 August – just 48 hours after the unit had returned to No 11 Group following a break from operations at Catterick.

Martel had made his first victory claim on 5 October in Spitfire I X4348, as he described in his post-mission Combat Report:

When on patrol with 603 Squadron I saw a circle of Me 109s, and one Me 109 left the circle and started to climb and I dived on him and made a beam attack, firing for about three seconds. The Me 109 took evasive action by skidding and I attacked again with slight deflection, firing the remainder of my

ABOVE Spitfire IIA P7325 served alongside P7350 at Wittering with No 266 Squadron in September 1940, both fighters being amongst the 18 F IIAs issued to the unit early in the month as replacements for its combat-weary F IAs. Lacking an individual aircraft identification letter, although marked with No 266 Squadron's 'UO' codes, P7325 'comes in over the hedge' at Wittering in September 1940. Like P7350, it too was transferred to No 603 Squadron on 17 October. (via Andy Thomas)

ammunition from 200 yards. The Messerschmitt went up and then dived gently into the sea. I saw him crash about six miles east of Dover.

During the morning of Friday, 25 October, No 603 Squadron scrambled 12 Spitfires from Hornchurch after German aircraft were detected approaching London. The first raid of the day consisted of three waves of aeroplanes, and occurred continuously between 0845–1030 hrs. Of an estimated 140 enemy aircraft detected over southeast England, 10–12 were Do 17 bombers in the first wave, while the rest of the aeroplanes were Bf 109s. Most of the enemy aircraft were confined to Kent, although some made it to London, where they dropped their bomb loads.

Amongst the No 603 Squadron aircraft desperately climbing for altitude through thick cloud in an attempt to get above the approaching German formations was P7350, flown by Pilot Officer Martel (oddly, the Pole has listed P7325 as the aircraft he was flying that day). Whilst gaining altitude, the Spitfire pilots were alarmed to hear over the radio that the fighter controller vectoring the squadron towards the enemy had been informed by radar plotters that there were already Bf 109s in their immediate vicinity. Moments later they received a second warning that the enemy aeroplanes were almost on top of them. As the 12 Spitfires finally broke through the overcast into clear blue skies at 25,000 ft, they were bounced by a gaggle of Bf 109s from *Jagdgeschwader* 51. Leading the Luftwaffe unit was high-scoring ace Major Werner Mölders.

ABOVE Pilot Officer Ludwik Martel – seen here in early 1941 after joining No 317 Squadron – was at the controls of P7350 (or, possibly, P7325) on the morning of Friday, 25 October 1940 when he was bounced from above by JG 51 at 25,000 ft and shot up. He managed to force land his engineless Spitfire near Hastings. (via John Dibbs)

No 603 Squadron immediately broke apart, with some pilots fighting to survive whilst others gave chase after the now disappearing Bf 109s. As befitting his status as one of the Luftwaffe's leading aces, Mölders' aim had been good during JG 51's solitary pass. He had targeted the last vic of three Spitfires, flown by Pilot Officers Peter Olver, John Soden and Ludwik Martel. Olver and Soden were both forced to bail out of their mortally damaged Spitfires over the Sussex/Kent border, having become Mölders' 63rd and 64th victims. Finally,

Having survived almost five years of service (which included being shot down once and damaged at least twice in accidents) with the RAF, a weather-beaten P7350 awaits its fate at No 39 MU at Slade's Farm in July 1948 – it had been in open-air storage for three years by then, hence its appearance. (via Peter R. Arnold)

RIGHT Following two years as No 92 Squadron Spitfire II 'QJ-K', flown by Pilot Officer Geoffrey Wellum during the Battle of Britain, P7350 became No 41 Squadron's 'EB-G' in 2011 in honour of Pilot Officer Eric 'Sawn Off' Lock – the highest scoring Spitfire pilot of the Battle of Britain. P7350's yellow gas detection patch and wing stiffening strakes (which began appearing retrospectively on Spitfires undergoing depot-level overhauls from October 1941) are clearly visible as the pilot performs a slow roll high over Lincolnshire. The strakes were introduced to Spitfire IAs, IIAs and VA/Bs (not VCs) that had seen considerable service – usually frontline, followed by OTUs – in an effort to stiffen the top skinning of the wings immediately over the wheel wells.

OPPOSITE P7350 has worn numerous Battle of Britain-related colour schemes during its many years with the Battle of Britain Memorial Flight, these regularly changing during each major overhaul. In 1999 the fighter was marked with the codes 'XT-D', representing the Spitfire flown by No 603 Squadron's CO during the summer of 1940, Squadron Leader George Denholm. In 2006 P7350 had its individual letter changed to 'W', as it was marked when flown by Pilot Officer Ludwik Martel in October 1940. This was changed to 'XT-L' in 2007 in honour of Gerald 'Stapme' Stapleton, whose Spitfire wore these codes during the Battle of Britain.

As the Battle of Britain Memorial Flight's only genuine Battle of Britain veteran, P7350 is arguably the most important aeroplane operated by the Flight. During the fighter's most recent major overhaul, in 2008–09, the Aircraft Restoration Company dismantled the Spitfire at its Duxford facility and installed new spars for both wings and sections of new skin where required.

LEFT 'Sawn Off Lockie' was credited with 23 victories between 15 August and 17 November 1940, when he was gravely wounded by a Bf 109E from 5./JG 54. Following seven months of convalescing, Lock briefly returned to No 41 Squadron before being posted to No 611 Squadron as a flight commander. Claiming three more victories (as seen here on his Spitfire VB at Hornchurch in late July 1941), Lock was posted missing in action on 3 August 1941 after failing to return from a mission over France. Neither his body nor his fighter, Spitfire VB W3257, were ever found. (via John Dibbs)

P7350's left wing was holed when a cannon shell was fired through it. Martel also heard banging noises behind him and then felt a sharp pain in the left side of his body and leg.

Diving back into cloud so as to shake off his unseen assailant, Martel then checked himself over for signs of where he had been wounded. There was little blood, but his leather flying jacket had been torn and he knew he had been hit in the left leg by shrapnel when the cannon shell that struck the fighter's wing had exploded. Unimpressed by the fact that he was now going to have to nurse his badly damaged Spitfire back through the thick cloud cover he had only just flown through minutes earlier, Martel struggled to concentrate on cockpit instruments as he descended. 'I lost consciousness', he recalled many years later, 'and when I came to I realised I was below the cloud upside down. There was a large hole in the left wing and my engine was not working'. Righting his aeroplane just above the ground, Martel force landed the machine in a grassy field near Hastings, in East Sussex.

When I looked out of the cockpit I saw a windmill. I had not seen one since arriving in England, and I knew that there were plenty of them in Holland. I now began to wonder if, while I was unconscious, I had flown across the North Sea. I feared that I

would be taken prisoner by German soldiers, but none came. Soon, a Home Guard patrol arrived – old grandpas, or so they seemed to me – but I was unable to communicate with them. Although I now knew that I was safely in England, the Home Guard thought that I was a German! Finally, an officer appeared and I was correctly identified as a pilot in the RAF. My wounds were dressed and I was taken to a hospital. I must have been suffering from a fever by then for I threatened to shoot a German flyer who had been admitted at the same time as me.

Following ten days recuperating, Martel returned to operations with No 603 Squadron on 6 November.

P7350, meanwhile, had suffered Category B damage (beyond repair on site, but repairable at a Maintenance Unit or at a contractor's works). Recovered shortly after its forced landing, the aeroplane was transported to No 1 Civilian Repair Unit at Cowley, in Oxford, on 31 October. The Spitfire had been repaired and was ready for collection by 7 December, on which date it was flown to No 37 MU at Burtonwood, in Lancashire, for 'service preparation' (the incorporation of the latest modifications and armaments) and subsequent storage. The fighter was then sent to No 616 'County of South Yorkshire' Squadron at Tangmere, in Sussex, on 18 March 1941 as an

OPPOSITE Literally hundreds of pilots have eased themselves into the snug confines of P7350's cockpit since it emerged from the Castle Bromwich 'Shadow Factory' in Birmingham in early 1940. Amongst the first to take the aeroplane aloft was legendary Spitfire test pilot Alex Henshaw, who flew the fighter from Collyweston, near Stamford, to Hornchurch on 17 October 1940 when it was transferred from No 266 Squadron to No 603 Squadron.

attrition replacement for a Spitfire II lost eight days earlier. On 10 April P7350 returned to Hornchurch when it was transferred to No 64 Squadron, again as an attrition replacement – the unit had lost a Spitfire II to II./JG 51 over the French coast the previous day.

The squadron moved north to Turnhouse, south of Edinburgh, on 16 May, and then on to Drem, in East Lothian, 24 hours later. On 5 August P7350 was sent to Scottish Aviation Ltd at Prestwick for overhaul and repair, being sent back to No 37 MU upon the completion of this work on 29 January 1942. No longer considered suitable for frontline service, the aeroplane spent the rest of the war fulfilling training roles with, initially, the Central Gunnery School, followed by No 57 OTU. It twice suffered Category B damage during this period, being repaired by Air Service Training Ltd at Hamble, in Hampshire, on both occasions. Placed in storage with No 39 MU at

Colerne, in Wiltshire, on 24 July 1945, and then moved to its satellite site at Slade's Farm, in Oxfordshire, the fighter was sold as scrap to John Dale & Sons Ltd on 8 July 1948. Upon receiving the aeroplane's log books, the company realised the historical importance of P7350 and presented it to RAF Colerne as a museum piece.

The aircraft remained here until March 1967, when it was moved to RAF Henlow, in Bedfordshire, to be restored to airworthiness for use by Spitfire Productions Ltd in the motion picture *The Battle of Britain*. Flown for the first time in more than two decades on 20 May 1968, the aeroplane was allocated to the Battle of Britain Memorial Flight (BBMF) in October of that year. Since then P7350 has been seen at numerous airshows and events across the UK, with its schemes regularly changing in keeping with the BBMF's policy of applying new markings during each major overhaul.

Spitfire F VC EE602 was rebuilt by The Spitfire Company Ltd of Biggin Hill, with structural work completed by VMI Engineering of Aldershot and Airframe Assemblies on the Isle of Wight.

CHAPTER TWO

SPITFIRE Mκ V

SPITFIRE F VC EE602

This aircraft was built by Westland in Yeovil, Somerset, as part of contract B124305/40 which called for the construction of 45 Spitfire VCs. Delivered to No 33 MU at Lyneham, in Wiltshire, on 11 September 1942, EE602 was issued to No 66 Squadron at nearby Zeals shortly thereafter. Equipped with both Spitfire VBs and rarer VCs at the time, the unit had been heavily involved in the disastrous Dieppe raid of 19 August that had seen the RAF lose 62 Spitfires – No 66 Squadron had had two Mk VCs downed by Fw 190s, with their pilots killed. The unit's operational strength was quickly restored, and led by its Kiwi CO, Squadron Leader Robert Yule (both a Battle of Britain veteran and an ace), No 66 Squadron remained heavily committed to flying convoy patrols, sweeps, bomber escort and 'Rhubarbs' (attacking targets of opportunity) from the No 10 Group airfields at Zeals, Warmwell (Dorset) and Ibsley (Hampshire).

EE602 flew its first mission with the unit on 1 October when Sergeant T. Hamer carried out a mundane convoy patrol that lasted 105 minutes. A further 30 operational sorties would be carried out by the aircraft in No 66 Squadron colours through to mid February 1943, when the fighter was transferred to No 129 'Mysore' Squadron. The highlight of this period was the bomber escort mission flown by the aircraft on 23 January 1943, with Rhodesian-born Flight Lieutenant George Elcombe at the controls. According to No 66 Squadron's Operations Record Book (ORB), 11 aircraft from the unit departed Exeter at 1325 hrs with 13 Spitfire VB/Cs from No 504 'County of Nottingham' Squadron and 11 Spitfire VIs from No 616 'South Yorkshire' Squadron. Making landfall at Ile-de-Bréhat, off the

No 66 Squadron's Sergeant Tim Hamer (seen here as a flight lieutenant) flew EE602 on its very first mission, from Zeals, on 1 October 1942 – a mundane convoy patrol off the south coast of England that lasted 105 minutes. (via Chris Fairfax)

Rhodesian-born Flight Lieutenant George Elcombe, who was one of No 66 Squadron's flight commanders in 1942–43, was credited with damaging an Fw 190 whilst flying EE602 on a bomber escort mission over Brittany on 23 January 1943. Elcombe, who had previously served as a sergeant pilot with No 266 Squadron in 1941–42, subsequently claimed four victories during the second half of 1943 flying Spitfire VIs with No 66 Squadron. He received a DFC in December 1943 in the wake of these successes. (via Chris Fairfax)

Flight Lieutenant Euan Watson (seen here shortly after being called up as a member of the RAF Volunteer Reserve on 1 September 1939, and before he had earned his pilot's wings) regularly flew EE602 following its transfer to No 129 Squadron in February 1943. A veteran of the Battle of Britain with No 64 Squadron, he had then spent time as an instructor with No 58 OTU prior to returning to the frontline with No 93 Squadron in June 1942. Watson became a flight commander with No 610 Squadron three months later, prior to joining No 129 Squadron. (via Chris Fairfax)

ABOVE During the morning of 31 May 1943, EE602 became a 'Presentation' Spitfire when it was handed over to No 129 Squadron by Brigadier F. D. Hammond, Chairman of the Central Uruguayan Railways Company, and Mrs Hammond in a brief ceremony held at Ibsley. Adorned with the titling "CENTRAL RAILWAYS URUGUAYAN STAFF" forward of the cockpit, the fighter was 'handed over' to No 129 Squadron's CO, Belgian Battle of Britain veteran Squadron Leader Henri Gonay (seen here second from left). Following lunch in the mess, Brigadier and Mrs Hammond were treated to a short flight demonstration of 'their' Spitfire, with Flight Lieutenant Watson (second from right) at the controls. (via Chris Fairfax)

OPPPOSITE Brigadier Hammond addresses senior officers from the Ibsley Wing and personnel from No 129 Squadron during the presentation ceremony for EE602. Standing to the left of Mrs Hammond is Wing Commander C. F. 'Bunny' Currant, Wing Commander Flying of the Ibsley Wing at that time. A high-scoring Hurricane ace during the Battle of Britain, Currant received a DSO five weeks after this photograph was taken. Note EE602's clipped wings, the fighter's wingtips having been removed just nine days earlier. Flight Lieutenant Watson took the aeroplane aloft for a 25-minute air test following this modification, and he subsequently noted in his log book, 'First time on clipped wing job – very nice. V's wings clipped – very good'. (via Chris Fairfax)

Brittany coast, 40 minutes later in a stepped up formation that topped off at 24,000 ft, the RAF fighters rendezvoused with the 'two boxes' of USAAF B-17F Flying Fortresses they had been charged with escorting near Morlaix as they headed for home.

Led by Battle of Britain ace Squadron Leader Harold Bird-Wilson, No 66 Squadron was detached from the rest of the Ibsley Wing to provide close escort for the B-17s, 73 of which had attacked the port at Lorient and the U-boat pens at Brest – five bombers had been lost to German fighters from 7./JG 2 during the mission. Flight Lieutant Elcombe, who would later claim four victories in 1943 flying Spitfire VIs with No 66 Squadron, provided the following account of the operation:

I was 'Blue 1' in No 66 Squadron, who with Nos 504 and 616 Squadrons (the Ibsley Wing) were rear cover for Fortresses ('Ramrod 48'). The wing, with No 504 Squadron leading, No 66 Squadron on the right and No 616 Squadron on the left, climbed to 24,000 ft, crossing the French coast at Pleubian. Soon after crossing the coast the bombers were reported ahead and to starboard at the same height. The wing turned to starboard, and Wing Commander Morgan [Battle of Britain ace Tom Dalton-Morgan] detailed No 66 Squadron to escort the bombers home as enemy aircraft were in the vicinity.

The squadron was flying on the starboard side of the bombers when Squadron Leader Bird-Wilson, leading Red section, spotted a Fw 190 attacking the bombers from port, head on, turning to port and diving underneath the squadron, but too far away for us to make contact. Then another Fw 190 was reported ahead, at the same height as the squadron, which was then 15 miles north of les Sept Iles [airfield]. I saw this Fw 190 climb ahead and above the bombers. My section was detailed by the CO to attack him. This enemy aircraft kept making feint attacks on the bombers. He then turned to port, making a diving head-on attack on the bombers. With my section behind me I dived, turning to port, and having a full deflection half-second burst. He was diving into the sun. I saw strikes on the starboard side of the fuselage and saw the enemy aircraft judder and steepen its dive. This was also seen by 'Blue 2' and 'Blue 4'. I claim this enemy aircraft as damaged.

On 9 February 1943 No 66 Squadron was posted north to Skaebrae, in the Orkney islands, for a period of rest, although EE602 remained at Ibsley and duly joined the unit's replacement, No 129

Squadron, four days later. Having flown down from Skaebrae, the new unit was equipped with Spitfire VB/Cs left behind by No 66 Squadron. Convoy patrols, 'Rodeos' (seek and destroy missions), 'Ramrods' (fighter sweeps) and 'Circuses' (daytime bomber attacks with heavy fighter escort) were flown on a near-daily basis from Ibsley and, briefly, Tangmere, as the spring weather improved conditions over France. EE602 was primarily flown by Battle of Britain veteran Flight Lieutenant Euan Watson during its time with No 129 Squadron, and he engaged Fw 190s with the fighter during 'Ramrod 64' on 16 April 1943. The Luftwaffe aircraft, from JG 2, had attacked USAAF B-24Ds targeting Brest harbour, downing three bombers. Watson's aim was poor, however, as he failed to hit any of the enemy aeroplanes.

EE602 witnessed history on 17 May when it participated in the escort of B-17F 41-24485, better known as *Memphis Belle*, as it became the first USAAF bomber to complete 25 missions. No 129 Squadron's ORB for that day described the operation as follows:

> After briefing at Portreath, the squadron flew with Nos 610 and 65 Squadrons as the withdrawal cover wing to about 170 Fortresses attacking Lorient. After patrolling over Morlaix the wing withdrew with the bombers, one section led by Flight Lieutenant Watson [again in EE602] staying behind to orbit the crew of a bomber that had bailed out about 20 miles off Start Point. Flight Lieutenant Watson released his dinghy and threw it into the sea, but it caught upon his tail unit and it was some minutes before he could free it.

Six days later EE602 and Flight Lieutenant Watson flew two back-to-back sorties off the French coast, as noted in the ORB:

> The morning was fine and clear and a shipping recce of four aircraft from 'B' Flight was led by Flight Lieutenant Watson over St Peter Port Harbour in Guernsey about half-a-mile northwest of Herm. As they were going into line astern to cross the harbour Sub-Lieutenant P. G. F. Mercer (attached

Upon its transfer to No 452 Squadron RAAF in June 1943, EE602 was frequently flown by 21-year-old Queenslander Flight Lieutenant Don Andrews. He is seen here (with his appropriately marked Spitfire XVI) as a wing commander whilst leading the Australian Wing at Matlaske, in Norfolk, in early 1945. (via Andy Thomas)

from the Fleet Air Arm) was heard to report that he could not get any boost and later that his throttle had jammed. The section turned to search for him but nothing was seen. As they proceeded north they sighted a convoy of some six ships steaming south westwards from Guernsey, and after a fix on their location was given they returned to base.

> The rest of the squadron was called to a hurried briefing and then led by the CO [Belgian Battle of Britain pilot Squadron Leader Henri Gonay], took off again – with three pilots from the previous operation – and eight aircraft from No 616 Squadron as the anti-flak unit. Both squadrons rendezvoused with four 'Whirlibombers' [from No 263 Squadron] to attack the convoy off Guernsey. A successful attack was made, with direct hits being scored by one of the bombers on one of the ships and three of our pilots firing at escort vessels – hits were seen on the bridge of the leading ship. Considerable return flak was experienced from both ships and land batteries. The squadron returned to breakfast after a busy morning and then put up three convoy patrols till rain and low cloud stopped play.

On 22 May, 24 hours before the convoy attack, EE602 had had its distinctive elliptical wings 'clipped' when the fighter's wingtips were removed outboard of the ailerons and replaced by shorter, squared-off fairings to improve low-altitude performance and enhance its roll rate – one area where the Spitfire V had fallen badly behind the rival Fw 190. Flight Lieutenant Watson had taken the aeroplane aloft for a 25-minute air test following

OPPOSITE EE602 made its first post-restoration flight from Biggin Hill on 16 May 2015, its elliptical wingtips firmly in place – as this underside view clearly shows.

this modification, and he subsequently noted in his log book, 'First time on clipped wing job – very nice. V's wings clipped – very good.'

The last day of May saw No 129 Squadron providing escort cover for six Ventura bombers mounting a mid-morning raid on targets in Cherbourg harbour. It appears that this operation did not involve the whole unit, as the ORB entry for the 31st explains:

During the course of the morning the squadron was honoured by the visit of Brigadier F. D. Hammond, Chairman of the Central Uruguayan Railways Company, and Mrs Hammond, the occasion marking the handing over of a Spitfire [EE602] aircraft purchased by donations from the Central Uruguayan Railway Company's staff. The ceremony was witnessed by a representative gathering of squadron personnel. The Brigadier, after being introduced to squadron officers, made a short speech in which he stated that the gift of the aircraft was a practical expression of Uruguayan sympathies with the Allied cause. Squadron Leader Gonay responded suitably and Brigadier and Mrs Hammond were entertained to lunch at the Mess, after which Flight Lieutenant Watson gave a short demonstration flight in the Spitfire.

The idea of 'Presentation' Spitfires (numerous other fighter and bomber types were also acquired in this way) was the brainchild of Minister of Aircraft Production, Lord Beaverbrook, in 1940. In an effort to raise much-needed funds to help Britain defend itself against Nazi attack, he promoted the idea that individuals, companies, clubs, even counties could 'buy their own Spitfire'. All they had to do was to collect £5,000 for their donation and a Spitfire would be named after them. That figure was plucked from the air by Beaverbrook, as the true cost of a Spitfire was in the region of £12,000. Nevertheless, the idea caught on like wildfire and the British people started collecting for 'their' Spitfire.

'Presentation' Spitfires also proved popular further afield in countries sympathetic with Britain's plight. One such group was the Central Uruguayan Railways Company, which was run at the time by British 'expats' who wanted to do something to help with the war effort. They duly raised the requisite £5,000 that saw EE602 adorned with the titling "CENTRAL RAILWAYS URUGUAYAN STAFF" forward of the cockpit. The fighter was also adorned with the emblem of a tiger morphing into a Spitfire immediately below the windscreen, this artwork almost certainly being inspired by No 129 Squadron's connection with the Maharaja

LEFT EE602 bears the titling "CENTRAL RAILWAYS URUGUAYAN STAFF" forward of the cockpit, the primarily 'expat' management of the Central Uruguayan Railways Company having raised the requisite £5,000 to pay for the fighter's construction as part of the 'Presentation' scheme promoted by the Minister of Aircraft Production, Lord Beaverbrook. The fighter was also adorned with the emblem of a tiger morphing into a Spitfire immediately below the windscreen.

of Mysore, who raised large sums of money for the war effort through the sale of War Bonds.

On 28 June No 129 Squadron was posted to Hornchurch, where it was to re-equip with Spitfire IXBs formerly assigned to No 453 Squadron of the Royal Australian Air Force (RAAF). The latter unit in turn inherited the Mk VB/Cs left behind at Ibsley by No 129 Squadron. With No 453 Squadron, EE602 was routinely flown by flight commander Flight Lieutenant Don Andrews, a 21-year-old Queenslander who had enlisted in the RAAF in November 1940. Having previously experienced combat with Nos 615, 245 and 175 Squadrons (all equipped with Hurricane IIs), Andrews was posted to No 453 Squadron as a replacement for Malta ace Flight Lieutenant Jack Yarra, who had been killed in action on 10 December

1942. Later made CO of the squadron, and eventually Wing Commander of the Australian Wing at Matlaske, in Norfolk, Andrews first flew EE602 operationally on 4 July (by which time the aeroplane wore the unique squadron code 'FU-?').

He and the fighter saw considerable action on 27 July, participating in two missions as reported in the No 453 Squadron ORB:

Squadron airborne 0809 hrs for Bradwell Bay [in Essex], arriving at 0850 hrs. The [Ibsley] Wing took part in a No 11 Group 'Ramrod', acting as escort cover for up to 12 Venturas bombing the coke ovens at Zeebrugge [in Belgium]. Rendezvoused with bombers over base at 1020 hrs and escorted them to target without incident. Bombing results seen to be excellent. Returned to base at 1145 hrs.

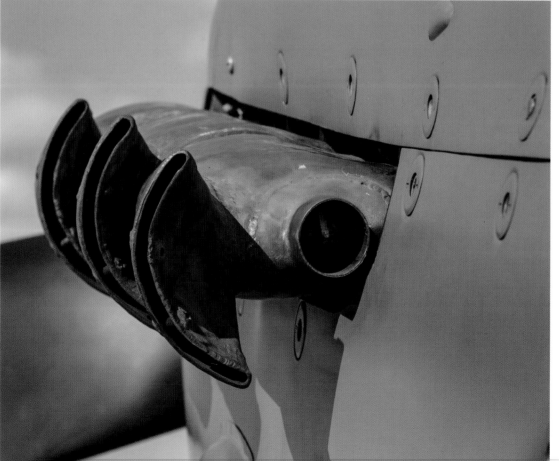

TOP Being a Spitfire VC, EE602 was built by Westland with the 'universal' C-type wing that was first tested on the Spitfire III prototype. The 'universal wing' was designed to reduce manufacturing time and allowed for three different armament options. The 'C' wing featured either eight 0.303-in machine guns, two 20 mm cannon and four 0.303-in machine guns or four 20 mm cannon. The Hispano Mk II cannon were belt-fed (using the Chattellerault system) from box magazines, which could hold 120 rounds per weapon. Like the 'B' wing before it, the 'C' wing had blisters on its upper-surfaces – in this case built into the gun bay covers to accommodate the cannon belt feed motors. Initially, a single, wide blister (as seen on EE602) was used to cover both cannon motors. Early-build Spitfire VCs were delivered with four 20 mm cannon, but two of these weapons were usually removed once the fighter was in frontline service. Later, production would shift back to the 'B' wing, with a single 20 mm cannon and four 0.303-in machine guns.

BOTTOM EE602 is powered by a Merlin 46 upgraded to 35 specification by Gloucestershire-based Retro Track and Air, as this is a much cleaner variant of the engine with greater reliability. The powerplant has been fitted with genuine fishtail exhaust stubs appropriate for such an early Merlin, including the heating pipe for the gun heating mechanism, which, as in the case of EE602, was usually disconnected by frontline squadrons.

The squadron, as part of the Ibsley Wing, left Bradwell Bay at 1520 hrs for Coltishall [Norfolk], arriving at 1550 hrs, and later took part in No 12 Group 'Ramrod' acting as escort cover for 12 Mitchells bombing Schlegel aerodrome. Rendezvoused with bombers over base and flew at 0 ft for 27 minutes, then climbed fast and crossed the Dutch coast at 14,000 ft. Approximately ten miles inland 6–8 ME 109s came suddenly out of the haze from slightly above and flew through the Wing, disappearing quickly in a dive into the haze again. Bombing results could not be observed and no further enemy aircraft seen. The squadron remained the night for another early morning show.

Flight Lieutenant Andrews and EE602 took part in another No 12 Group 'Ramrod' from Coltishall the following morning when No 453 Squadron flew close escort for 12 Bostons bombing Amsterdam. Again, the enemy coast was approached at sea level, before a fast climb to 11,000 ft. Bombing results were rated as 'fairly good'. Heading to Tangmere, in Sussex, later that same day, the unit was briefed to escort 18 Marauders targeting Triqueville [in France]. However, the bombers were late reaching the rendezvous point at Beachy Head and the operation was aborted. After staying the night, No 453 Squadron departed for Martlesham Heath, in Suffolk, at dawn on 29 July and was subsequently released for training later that day.

What proved to be EE602's final two missions came on 30 and 31 July, with Flying Officer Russ Ewins at the controls – the aeroplane appears to have been shared by Andrews and Ewins throughout the month. On the 30th the unit helped No 616 Squadron escort 21 Marauders on a 'Ramrod' to Woenndrecht, in Holland. The bombers were attacked by 15–20 Fw 190s from I./JG 26, and at least one Marauder was shot down. Several No 616 Squadron pilots engaged the enemy fighters, claiming one damaged, but No 453 Squadron failed to intercept the German aircraft.

The following day the unit flew down to Biggin Hill, and from there on to Manston, in Kent, to participate in another 'Ramrod' mission undertaken by 20 Marauders. Attacking Merville airfield, in France, the aeroplanes dropped their bombs unmolested, despite reports of enemy fighters both north and south of the target. Once the bombers had cleared the enemy coast, No 453 Squadron returned to Manston to refuel and then headed back to Martlesham Heath. Later that same day the unit returned to Ibsley, although Flying Officer Ewins remained behind at the Suffolk airfield to have EE602's tail wheel changed. Shortly thereafter, an unidentified aircraft taxied into the Spitfire and wrote it off. The fighter was subsequently abandoned at Martlesham Heath, having flown more than 100 missions in nine months of uninterrupted frontline operations.

The fighter's remains were eventually discovered by a warbird collector in an Australian scrap-yard that had dismantled numerous Spitfires post-war, EE602 having likely been reduced to components shortly after it was declared Category E (written off). These parts were then taken to Australia by No 453 Squadron for use as spares. Eventually returned to the UK, along with components from another Spitfire, EE602 was acquired by Fairfax Spitfires LLP in January 2012 and its rebuild overseen by The Spitfire Company Ltd of Biggin Hill. Structural work was completed by VMI Engineering of Aldershot and Airframe Assemblies on the Isle of Wight, while Gloucestershire-based Retro Track and Air restored the engine – the Merlin 46 fitted to the fighter was upgraded to 35 specification to give EE602 greater reliability. Systems and component (many of the latter predating the fighter's September 1942 build date) fitting was undertaken by Peter Monk and his team at Biggin Hill from April 2014, culminating in the Spitfire making its first post-restoration flight from the famous No 11 Group fighter station on 16 May 2015.

MT719's Merlin 66 proved to be too badly corroded for restoration, so a 1740 hp Merlin 114A removed from Mosquito TT 35 TA634 (an exhibit in Mosquito Aircraft Museum since 1970) was installed instead – this work was carried out by legendary warbird engineer Pete Rushen, then still serving in the RAF with the Battle of Britain Memorial Flight.

CHAPTER THREE

SPITFIRE Mκ VIIIs

SPITFIRE LF VIII MT719

O rdered from Supermarine Aviation (Vickers) Ltd on 27 July 1942, MT719 emerged from the company's Southampton factory in June 1944. Taken on charge by No 9 MU at Cosford on 21 June, the fighter was transferred to No 215 MU at Dumfries on 10 July and taken to Glasgow docks the following day for shipment to Bombay on board the SS *Turkestan*. Departing Glasgow on 28 July and arriving in Bombay on 5 September, being issued shortly thereafter to No 17 Squadron at Vavuniya and China Bay, in Ceylon. Amongst the pilots to fly the aircraft was Flight Lieutenant Don Healey, who had experienced combat in both Hurricanes and Spitfires in the Middle East prior to being sent to India:

MT719 had arrived on the squadron from Bombay in late 1944. It was subsequently flown on ops by Flight Sergeant Rex de Silva, the unit's sole Ceylonese pilot. The unit had previously been flying Hurricane IICs, and the new Spitfire VIIIs made such an impression on de Silva that he noted in his logbook, 'I picked up the new "J" today, coded MT719, and what a red hot machine it is!' He proceeded to fly it with A Flight well into early 1945. By May, it was fairly knackered, as Rex noted in his log book – 'Poor old "J" is coming to the end of its life, having refused to start this morning'.

Because of the rough nature of our airstrips, and constant flying at full throttle, a Spitfire rarely lasted more than six weeks in the frontline, with undercarriage failure, and the resulting ground loop, being one of the major wreckers of aircraft. If a machine saw more than two months' service, it was doing well.

We also got through engines at an alarming rate. I only began to realise how many aircraft we went through many years after the war when I was trying to tie up serials in log books with squadron maintenance records – we had five 'YB-Ts' in as many months! At the time one didn't really think too much about how hard Burma was on Spitfires. MT719 had done well to last as long as it had done.

In May the fighter went to No 3 Repair and Salvage Unit [RSU] and had its old Merlin engine swapped for a new one. The aeroplane was still with the RSU when I arrived back at No 17 Squadron's base at Thedaw from Rangoon, having represented the unit in the victory march through the Burmese capital on 15 June 1945. I soon discovered that the squadron had flown to Madura, in India, while I was

away in order to convert to Spitfire XIVs. No 909 Wing boss, Group Captain Donald Finlay, had also taken part in the march, and he told all 13 of us pilots from various squadrons who had been left behind to represent the RAF in the procession to grab an aircraft each from the RSU – they had Spitfires, Hurricanes, Beaufighters, Mosquitos and Thunderbolts – and fly back to India. I chose MT719.

Our 'rag tag' air force duly left Burma, and at each refuelling stop someone got left behind due to a technical snag – a fate that eventually struck me down at Visakhapatnam, on the east coast of India, when I suffered carburettor problems. I was accommodated in the Sultan's palace for several days while we found someone to adjust the engine, and I then pressed on to Madura.

ABOVE LEFT A 40 mm Bofors gun provides protection from attack as No 17 Squadron Spitfire VIII 'YB-M' is serviced at Sapam, in Burma. Canadian ace Flying Officer Don Rathwell was flying this machine on 14 February 1945 when he attacked a radial-engined enemy aircraft that he later thought might have been a Harvard, although this would appear to be unlikely. It was almost certainly a Ki-43 'Oscar'. (via J. D. R. Rawlings)

ABOVE Squadron Leader 'Ginger' Lacey, CO of No 17 Squadron, smiles for the camera shortly after shooting down a Ki-43 on 19 February 1945 for his 28th, and last victory. This proved to be his only success against the Japanese. (via C. F. Shores)

MT719 was flown by a number of pilots during its lengthy service with No 17 Squadron, including Warrant Officer O. J. F. Travers, who claimed an 'Oscar' probably destroyed on 24 February 1945 whilst flying 'YB-N' – he noted in his logbook that he was at the controls of MT719 just four days later. Whilst covering 4th Corps, Travers and Kiwi pilot Flying Officer Ken Rutherford spotted 14 Ki-43s strafing advancing armoured columns at Pakokku. They were successfully driven off by the No 17 Squadron pilots. As per standard RAF practice, Travers' logbook has been signed by his CO, Squadron Leader 'Ginger' Lacey, after the summary of his month's flying activity.

MT719 was subsequently flown by No 151 OTU from Peshawar and Ambala until it was sold to the Indian Air Force (IAF). Following the invasion of Jammu and Kashmir by Pakistani troops in October 1947 (which soon escalated into the first Indo-Pakistani War) the fighter was flown to Srinagar as part of No 1 Ad Hoc Squadron. The latter was equipped with Spitfire VIIIs and XIVs and Harvard IIBs hastily deployed from the Advanced Flying School at Ambala. From Srinagar, the unit would fly strafing missions against enemy forces, as well as myriad offensive reconnaissance sorties. Amongst the pilots flying Spitfire VIIIs during this bloody conflict was instructor Flying Officer Dilbagh Singh (who eventually became the IAF's Chief of the Air Staff in the early 1980s):

On 26 November I was asked to load up my Spitfire at Ambala and immediately fly to Jammu, as the fall of Mirpur seemed imminent. I was briefed by the ground liaison officer at Jammu and arrived over Mirpur to an unforgettable sight. About three-quarters of the town was burning, with naked dead bodies littering the streets. To the south, the invaders poured in, and the north, the pathetic men, women and children were trying to flee. For almost 20 minutes I strafed the enemy until I ran out of ammunition. By then the whole town was ablaze. All I could write in my log book after this mission was that I was a helpless witness to the fall of Mirpur.

Eventually retired in the early 1950s, MT719 was passed on to No 1 Rajasthan (Air) National Cadet Corps (NCC) Squadron at Sanganer, south of Jaipur. The fighter was one of eight Spitfires put up for sale by tender by the Indian Government in 1977. When inspected by Ormond and Wensley Haydon-Baillie, the aeroplane was found to be in reasonable condition. The airframe was parked outside a hangar at Jaipur, whilst its Merlin 66 engine, propeller and spinner ·were discovered inside the same hangar. By the time the fighter arrived at Wroughton in the spring of 1978, Ormond Haydon-Baillie had been killed in the crash of his Mustang. Wensley duly sold MT719 to Italian enthusiast Franco Actis, who had it shipped to Turin in December 1979. It took almost three years to restore the aeroplane to airworthiness, with its final assembly being undertaken by SIAI-Marchetti in Milan. On 27 October 1982, MT719, resplendent in the No 17 Squadron scheme worn by the fighter in 1944–45, completed its first post-restoration flight from SIAI-Marchetti's airfield at Vergiate.

In April 1989 the aeroplane was sold to Reynard Racing Cars Ltd of Bicester, in Oxfordshire, MT719 being based in the UK for four years until sold to the Cavanaugh Flight Museum of Dallas, Texas, in the summer of 1993. The fighter has been maintained in airworthy condition at the museum's Addison Airport facility ever since.

Restored in Italy in the early 1980s, MT719 was camouflaged in the No 17 Squadron colours it wore in Burma and India in 1944–45. Owned by the Cavanaugh Flight Museum of Dallas, Texas, since the summer of 1993, the fighter has remained airworthy – and in this scheme – ever since.

SPITFIRE HF VIII MV154

Built as part of Contract No 11877/C23, which covered the construction of both Mk VIII and Mk XIV Spitfires, MV154 was almost certainly manufactured at Supermarine Aviation (Vickers) Ltd's works in Southampton. It was flown to No 6 MU at Brize Norton on 15 September 1944 by Air Transport Auxiliary pilot Mary Wilkins, who signed the cockpit door – she autographed many of the 1,000 aeroplanes (including 400 Spitfires) that she delivered during World War 2. Her signature was subsequently found during MV154's restoration almost 50 years later, and Mary Ellis (née Wilkins) was reunited with the aeroplane.

Selected for service in Australia with the RAAF, MV154 was transferred from Brize Norton to No 82 MU's Preparation and Packing Depot at Lichfield, in Staffordshire, on 27 September 1944 for crating. The aeroplane subsequently arrived at Newport docks, in South Wales, three days later and eventually sent to Sydney (NSW) onboard the MV *Port Fairey* on 15 October. Upon arriving in New South Wales on 24 November, the aeroplane

was transferred to No 2 Aircraft Depot in Richmond shortly thereafter. Allocated the serial A58-671 on 9 December, the aeroplane was one of 120 Spitfires placed directly into store and never removed from its crate. Inspected on 22 March 1946, the fighter was eventually offered for disposal on 24 May 1948. Shortly thereafter Mark Leech, who was employed as an instructor at the Sydney Technical College, negotiated the donation of two Spitfire HF VIIIs (MV154 and MV239), a Vultee Vengeance and a Mosquito for use as teaching aids for aircraft apprentices.

The Spitfires and the Vengeance, all of which were still in their shipping crates, were moved from Richmond to the college in Ultimo, NSW. The Mosquito was not collected, however, due to it being in a damaged state. MV154 was assembled by the college, while MV239 (which also survived, and is presently a valued flying exhibit within the Temora Aviation Museum collection in NSW) remained in its crate in external storage. Components from the aeroplane were also used in the assembly of MV154. In 1961 the college exchanged both Spitfires for former RAAF Gloster Meteor F 8 A77-868 that had been acquired by former de Havilland Aircraft test pilot Squadron Leader A. J. R. 'Titus' Oates. The latter, who had been awarded a DFC whilst flying Beauforts with the RAAF in the South Pacific in 1943, was hoping to restore MV154 as a

LEFT No 145 Squadron primarily used the Spitfire VIII as a dive-bomber in support of Allied troops slugging it out with the Wehrmacht as they attempted to push the enemy back into northern Italy. Photographed taking off from Fano on just such a sortie in September 1944, this aeroplane is armed with a solitary Medium Capacity (MC) Mk I 250-lb bomb. Three of these could be carried by the Spitfire, or two (one under each wing) and a single MC Mk III 500-lb weapon (under the fuselage). The MC Mk III was the principal air-to-ground weapon carried by the Spitfire. (via Norman Franks)

BOTTOM Malta-based No 145 Squadron was the first frontline unit in the RAF to receive Spitfire VIIIs in June 1943. The squadron had moved to Italy by the time this photograph was taken in the summer of 1944, when legendary ace and future test pilot Squadron Leader Neville Duke was CO. Flight commander Flight Lieutenant Frankie Banner is posing with this clean HF VIII – he was later killed testing a Seafire for Supermarine. (via Norman Franks)

ABOVE Squadron Leader Neville Duke became CO of No 145 Squadron in March 1944, by which time the unit had accrued considerable combat experience with the Spitfire III. Having claimed 21 victories in three marks of Spitfire, Tomahawk IIBs and Kittyhawk IAs during frontline tours on the Channel Front and in North Africa, Duke was himself a veteran aviator with three years of combat behind him. He was very impressed with the Spitfire LF VIIIs, a mark that he had not previously flown prior to joining No 145 Squadron. 'To my mind the LF VIII was one of the finest marks of Spitfire ever produced', he later stated. He also claimed his final six aerial victories in the aeroplane. (via Norman Franks)

memorial to Battle of Britain pilots. The aircraft were moved to Bankstown airport, in NSW, where MV154 was reassembled. When the memorial plan fell through, both fighters were acquired by pioneer warbird collector Syd Marshall of Marshall Airways for display in his private museum.

MV154 returned to the UK in December 1979 after being sold to Robs Lamplough earlier that year. The aircraft was eventually sent to Charfield, in Gloucestershire, for restoration to airworthiness by volunteers from the Bristol Plane Preservation Unit and British Aerospace, Filton. Final assembly took place at the Filton site, in Bristol, and MV154 made its first flight in almost 50 years on 28 May 1994. Displayed at numerous airshows since then, and having been seen in two feature-length films (*Pearl Harbor* and *Dark Blue World*), MV154 was sold to Max Alpha Aviation GmbH/Meier Motors GmbH in February 2010.

Based in Bremgarten, Germany, since then, the fighter has retained the No 145 Squadron colour scheme applied by Robs Lamplough during its restoration. It bears the serial MT928, which was an LF VIII that served with Nos 451, 145 and 92 Squadrons prior to being struck off charge in March 1946. During its spell with No 145 Squadron at Bellaria, in Italy, in 1945, MT928 was flown by Flight Lieutenant G. R. S. McKay – he

later became the final wartime CO of No 87 Squadron. A high-scoring fighter unit credited with 224 aerial victories by war's end, No 145 Squadron had been the first to operate the Spitfire VIII, when based on Malta during June 1943. In March of the following year high-scoring ace Squadron Leader Neville Duke became CO. Having claimed 21 victories in three marks of Spitfire, Tomahawk IIBs and Kittyhawk IAs during frontline tours on the Channel Front and in North Africa, he was a veteran aviator with three years of combat behind him.

Duke was very impressed with No 145 Squadron's Spitfire LF VIIIs, which he had not previously flown. 'To my mind the LF VIII was one of the finest marks of Spitfire ever produced', he wrote in his autobiography, *Test Pilot*. 'They carried two 20 mm cannon, four 0.303-in machine guns, were fitted with Merlin 45 or 46 engines and could more than hold their own with the Me 109 and the Fw 190, although the "long-nose" Focke-Wulf with the Daimler-Benz engine was a formidable aircraft'.

Duke would claim his final six victories whilst flying Spitfire LF VIIIs with No 145 Squadron between 13 May and 3 September 1944, all of these kills being Bf 109Gs or Fw 190s. He described the last of these successes in the following extract from *Test Pilot*:

Photographed on the ramp at Filton shortly after completing the first post-restoration flight in his Spitfire VIII MV154 on 28 May 1994, Robs Lamplough is joined by Air Transport Auxiliary pilot Mary Ellis (née Wilkins). Almost 50 years earlier she had flown the fighter from Supermarine Aviation's Southampton works to No 6 MU at Brize Norton. (Peter R. Arnold)

Mary Ellis (née Wilkins) signed MV154's cockpit door – she autographed many of the 1,000 aeroplanes (including 400 Spitfires) that she delivered during World War 2. Her signature was subsequently found during the fighter's restoration, and she added a second one on the opposite side of the cockpit.

Accompanied by Flying Officer J. Hamer as my No 2, I took off before dawn to patrol the battle area between Pesaro and Rimini. There was nothing to be seen over the battle area, and not wishing to attract our own ack-ack, we flew north of Ancona along the coast at about 10,000 ft. Control reported two bogeys northwest of Pesaro, 3,000 ft above us. We missed them in cloud but picked them up north of Rimini – three 109s flying in line abreast.

All three put on full boost immediately they saw us, clouds of black smoke coming from their engines. Hamer and I went after them, and when the port aircraft lagged slightly I opened up at long range – about 600 to 800 yards – producing a bright flash on his fuselage. After I had drawn closer and fired again, the hood of the 109 flew off and out came the pilot. The two remaining Germans dived and then climbed steeply to 14,000–15,000 ft – a height at which we were able to use the Spitfire VIII's supercharger, allowing us to catch them easily. I selected one and, firing from long range, closed to 200 yards. The aircraft caught fire and again the pilot bailed out. The third 109 disappeared.

These two successes took Neville Duke's final tally of aerial victories to 26 and 2 shared kills.

Having never been removed from its packing crate following shipment to Australia in the autumn on 1944, and therefore possessing no wartime history, MV154 has been marked up as MT928 of No 145 Squadron since its return to airworthiness more than 20 years ago. MT928 served with Nos 451, 145 and 92 Squadrons prior to being struck off charge in March 1946. During its spell with No 145 Squadron at Bellaria, in Italy, in 1945, the fighter was flown by Flight Lieutenant G. R. S. McKay, who later became the final wartime CO of No 87 Squadron.

MH434 effortlessly flies over thickening cloud during a photo sortie from its Duxford base, the Spitfire's Dark Green and Ocean Grey day fighter camouflage scheme, Type C roundels, Sky spinner, fuselage band and code letters and three-colour roundel contrasting markedly with the cloudscape behind it.

CHAPTER FOUR

MH434

SPITFIRE LF IXB MH434

Arguably the most famous airworthy Spitfire in the world thanks to its many years as a regular fixture on the British airshow circuit, MH434 was built in early August 1943 at Castle Bromwich as part of Contract No 981687/39 covering the manufacture of 2,190 Mks V, IX and XVI aircraft. Test flown by Alex Henshaw, the aeroplane was delivered to No 222 'Natal' Squadron at Hornchurch and was in service by 19 August. The fighter was assigned to 'A' Flight CO Flight Lieutenant Pat Lardner-Burke, the South African pilot having 'made ace' flying Hurricanes in defence of Malta with No 126 Squadron in 1941. Badly wounded in action in November 1941, Lardner-Burke was finally deemed fit enough to return to the frontline in March 1943 when he joined No 222 Squadron at Ayr, in Scotland, just prior to it returning to No 11 Group.

The unit had swapped its Spitfire VBs for Mk IXs when it moved to Hornchurch from Martlesham Heath in late April 1943, the squadron subsequently receiving brand new Merlin 66-powered LF IXBs (including MH434) four months later. Lardner-Burke would enjoy some success with No 222 Squadron, claiming 2.5 kills and one damaged in MH434 in the space of just 11 days. The first of these came on 27 August during an escort mission for Eighth Air Force B-17s targeting a V-weapons site at Watten for the first time, the details of the operation being described in the Hornchurch Wing's Intelligence Form 'F' lodged with the Intelligence Branch of HQ Fighter Command three days later:

The Wing, led by Wing Commander W. V. Crawford-Compton, and consisting of 26 Spitfire IXBs (13 of No 222 Squadron, including the Wing Leader, and 13 from No 129 Squadron) took off from base at 1833 hrs detailed to act as high fighter cover to the third force of 60 Fortresses attacking a target four miles north of St Omer marshalling yards.

The Wing climbed from base, crossed out over Dungeness at 16,000 ft at 1850 hrs, made French landfall and rendezvoused with the bombers over Berck at 1904 hrs, having reached 22,000 ft and positioned themselves to port of the leading box of Fortresses. After reaching a point northwest of St Pol, the formation turned left and flew due north to St Omer and then on to Mardyck. Having escorted the first box about 15 miles out to sea, the Wing turned back to St Omer, picked up another box of bombers, escorted them out and then returned to pick up the third box. When between St Omer and Mardyck on the third time out at 1939 hrs, nine FW 190s [from JG 2 and JG 26] were seen diving on the bombers in loose small formation and then coming up beneath them. While Red Section of No 129 Squadron and Yellow Section of No 222 Squadron remained above as cover, the rest of the Wing were led down to attack, engaging the enemy at 15,000 ft. Combats took place between this height and 5,000 ft, resulting in

LEFT South African Flight Lieutenant Pat Lardner-Burke joined No 222 Squadron as 'A' Flight Commander in March 1943, just prior to the unit being posted from Ayr to Martlesham Heath, and then on to Hornchurch. From late August of that year Lardner-Burke, who had 'made ace' in the defence of Malta in 1941, started routinely flying MH434. He would claim 2.5 victories and one damaged in the fighter in the space of just 11 days. (via Chris Yeoman)

three FW 190s being destroyed and one damaged by No 222 Squadron.

Red 3, Flight Lieutenant H. P. Lardner-Burke, saw a FW 190 attack Red 1 and 2 (Wing Commander Compton and Wing Commander Davidson) and, getting on its tail, fired a two-second burst from 350–300 yards. He saw strikes on the starboard wing and tail of the enemy aircraft, which then turned sharply starboard and dived away. This was seen by Red 1 and 2 and enemy aircraft is claimed as damaged.

Red 3 then attacked another FW 190, closing to 300 yards and firing a four-second burst from five degrees off dead astern. The enemy aircraft dived and Red 3, following it, fired a two-second burst from astern at 300 yards, resulting in the enemy aircraft diving vertically into the ground near Audricq. This was witnessed by Red 4 and Yellow 2 and 3, and the enemy aircraft is claimed destroyed.

After the engagement, our aircraft withdrew in small formation and one landed at Gravesend, the remainder landing at base by 2017 hrs.

Flight Lieutenant Lardner-Burke and MH434 met the enemy again on 5 September, as noted in the Intelligence Form 'F' for the operation:

The Wing, comprising 12 Spitfire IXBs from No 222 Squadron and led by Wing Commander W. V. Crawford-Compton and 13 Spitfire IXBs from No 129 Squadron, took off from base at 0742 hrs as high cover to 72 Marauders detailed to attack the marshalling yards at Ghent/Meirelbeke.

Rendezvous was made on time (0800 hrs) at North Foreland and, after climbing from there, the beehive reached Knocke, flew along the coast and crossed at Nieuwe Sluis at 0816 hrs at 21,000 ft. The Wing was warned of enemy aircraft approaching from the northeast, and therefore orbited over Sas van Ghent and later east of Ghent, where bombs were seen to burst on the marshalling yards and in the town at 0829 hrs. After turning to starboard from the target and when approaching Nieuport at 0840 hrs, the Wing was bounced by about 20 FW 190s [from JG 26] out of the sun. Red and Yellow sections of No 222 Squadron and Red and Blue sections of No 129 Squadron engaged the enemy aircraft and many combats took place.

No 222 Squadron's Yellow section climbed to port to head off ten FW 190s. One of these turned in front of Flight Lieutenant H. P. Lardner-Burke (Yellow 1), who fired a three-second burst from about 500–450 yards, five degrees off. The enemy aircraft did a quick

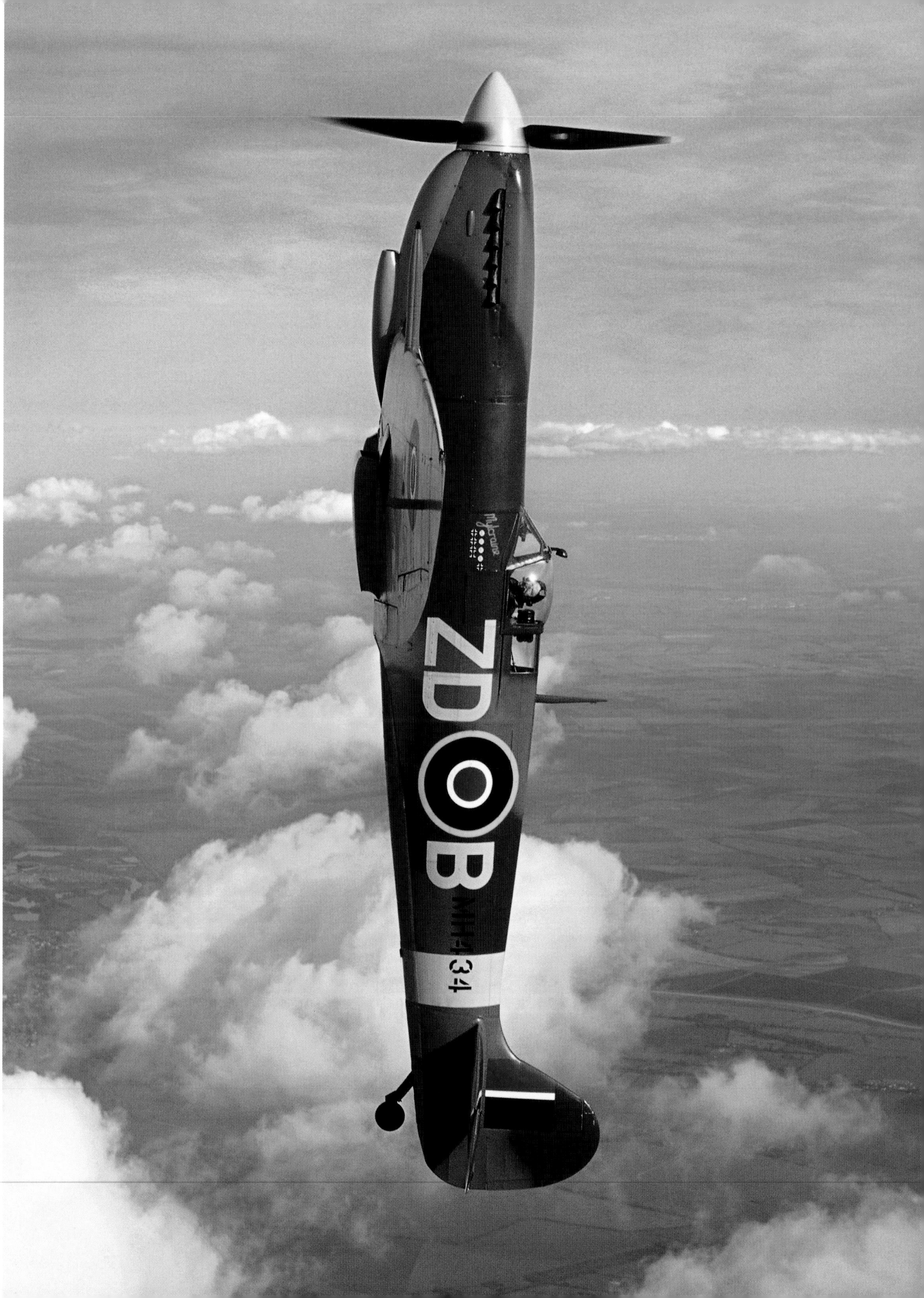
ZD B
MH434

roll and Yellow 1 followed with another three-second burst from 400 yards astern, scoring hits on the engine and cockpit. This was seen by Yellow 2, flying line abreast, and by Yellow 3 and 4, who also observed an explosion in the cockpit and the enemy aircraft turn over, pouring smoke, and then go down on fire and in an uncontrolled spin.

The enemy coast was finally left at 0850 hrs between Nieuport and Dunkirk.

According to this report, Lardner-Burke had fired 132 20 mm cannon rounds and 274 0.303-in machine gun rounds in three three-second bursts to down the Fw 190.

MH434's final aerial success came on 8 September when the Hornchurch Wing again provided high cover for USAAF B-17s, the Intelligence Form 'F' for the mission noting:

The Hornchurch Wing, comprising 25 Spitfire IXBs (13 from No 222 Squadron, including Wing Commander W. V. Crawford-Compton, and 12 from No 129 Squadron), was airborne at 1715 hrs, the object being to provide high cover to a formation of bombers bombing targets in the Boulogne area between 1740 hrs and 1817 hrs. The Wing was led by Squadron Leader H. A. C. Gonay of No 129 Squadron because the wing commander was unable to take off at the appointed time due to engine trouble. However, he followed in another aircraft, arriving in the target area shortly after the Wing.

The French coast was crossed just north of Hardelot at 22,000 ft at 1740 hrs. Three patrols were made between Headin and Audricq, No 222 Squadron flying at 24,000 ft. No 129 Squadron flew 1,000 ft above and between No 222 Squadron and the coast.

At the end of the third patrol at 1757 hrs, 12 Me 109Fs were sighted by No 222 Squadron, which was then at 25,000 ft. These enemy aircraft were just changing onto a southwesterly course from a northwesterly course from St Omer, just south of St Omer. The enemy aircraft on sighting No 222 Squadron climbed, with the exception of two Me 109Fs which dived. No 222 Squadron broke to port, Blue section going down.

Flight Lieutenant H. P. Lardner-Burke and Flying Officer O. Smik (Blue 1 and 2) dived down on the leading enemy aircraft, which was diving steeply to the southeast, while Blue 3 and 4 followed, covering their attack. Flight Lieutenant Lardner-Burke opened fire from about ten degrees, closing to dead astern at 350–300 yards range. He fired two bursts of three seconds and one of two seconds. Black smoke was seen to pour from the enemy aircraft, which appeared to be in difficulties. Flight Lieutenant Lardner-Burke broke to port to enable Flying Officer Smik to fire a 14-second burst from 300 yards dead astern, closing to 250 yards. He expended all of his ammunition and broke off the combat at 7,000 ft. The enemy aircraft continued to dive at about 500 mph. Both Blue 1 and 2 were diving at 470/480 mph. The starboard wingtip of the enemy aircraft fell off and it dived straight into the ground 10–15 miles south-southeast of Boulogne. The crash was also witnessed by Flying Officer Wyllie (Blue 3).

The wing crossed out between Hardelot and Boulogne at 1820 hrs at 20,000 ft. All aircraft had landed at base by 1850 hrs.

Although Flight Lieutenant Lardner-Burke was transferred out to HQ Fighter Command at Stanmore, in Middlesex, in October 1943, MH434 remained with No 222 Squadron until the unit was sent north to Woodvale, in Lancashire, on 30 December. The fighter was left behind at Hornchurch for No 350 'Belgian' Squadron, which had transferred in from Hawkinge, in Kent, and swapped its Spitfire VB/Cs in the process. This proved to be only a temporary switch, however, for No 222 Squadron returned to Hornchurch in March 1944 and MH434 rejoined the unit when No 350 Squadron headed back to Hawkinge, and Spitfire VB/Cs.

On 15 June the fighter was allocated to No 84 Group Support Unit (GSU), which held aircraft and pilots for the operational squadrons in Nos 83 and 84 Groups, which were in turn part of the 2nd Tactical Air Force. They maintained a large number (circa 90) of aircraft of all types used by the squadrons in each group,

MH434 has worn myriad schemes during its 60 years of civilian ownership, including two that honoured Polish Air Force units serving with the RAF in World War 2. The first of these saw the fighter temporarily marked up with No 316 Squadron codes and adorned with the personal markings of ace Wing Commander Aleksander Gabszewicz when wing leader of No 2 Polish Wing in the second half of 1943. It wore these markings from May 1997 through to June 1998. Here, Ray Hanna's son Mark performs a typically spirited display in MH434 at Shuttleworth.

MH434 is one of the world's most original airworthy Spitfires, the fighter undergoing its first – and so far only – major rebuild whilst in civilian ownership during the winter of 1994–95 with the Aircraft Restoration Company at Duxford.

prepared ready for issue to these units to replace losses. They also had conversion flights to provide type conversion and continuation training for the pool of pilots that were posted to the GSUs to await demand for replacement from the frontline squadrons. The instructors serving with the GSUs were usually pilots 'resting' between operational tours.

MH434 appears to have remained with No 84 GSU for the rest of its active life with the RAF. Damaged in December 1944, it spent four months being repaired by Air Service Training Ltd only to then be placed in storage with No 9 MU at Cosford, in Shropshire, on 2 May 1945. Transferred to No 76 MU at Wroughton, in Wiltshire, on 27 July 1946 for disposal, MH434 was one of a large number of Spitfires sold to the Royal Netherlands Air Force (RNAF) on 19 February 1947. Shipped from Tilbury docks on 19 May, the fighter never actually saw any service in Holland. It was one of 20 aircraft transported to Batavia, in the Dutch East Indies, where it became the first Spitfire to be reassembled and test flown from Kalidjati air base on 31 October 1947.

Assigned to No 322 Squadron, MH434 flew 165 missions against Nationalist forces in Java from 22 December 1947. It dropped 50 250-lb bombs in anger, as well as food and medical containers for Dutch troops. The fighter was also engaged in strafing Nationalist targets. Damaged in a belly landing on 15 April 1949 when its pilot ran out of fuel (the fighter was also suffering from hydraulic failure), MH434 was soon repaired. When the Dutch withdrew from Indonesia the aircraft was placed in storage in Andir, and then shipped back to Holland in July 1950. Stored at Rotterdam docks for some time, the aeroplane was sold to the Belgian Air Force (BAF) along with 14 other Spitfires on 30 April 1952. Acquired as attrition replacements, the veteran fighters were overhauled by Fokker NV at Schiphol airport – MH434 was delivered to the BAF on 9 October 1953. Serving briefly as a fighter trainer with *L'École de Chasse* at Brustem, the aeroplane was damaged on 19 March 1954 and eventually struck off charge seven months later.

MH434 was eventually acquired by COGEA Nouvelle (which bought six ex-BAF Spitfire IXs, five of which are in existence today) in March 1956 and placed on the Belgian civil registry, the Spitfire being used as a target-towing aircraft for the BAF from Ostend. In 1963 MH434 was bought by Tim Davies and flown back to the UK, the fighter being overhauled at Elstree, in Hertfordshire, by Simpson's Aeroservices Ltd. Initially flown from here with clipped wings, the aeroplane soon had its elliptical wingtips refitted to allow the Spitfire to operate with greater safety margins from Elstree's short runway.

In November 1967 MH434 was acquired by Spitfire Productions for *The Battle of Britain* film, and following completion of the motion picture it was sold to Sir Adrian Swire on 27 June 1969. The fighter would remain in his ownership until sold at Christie's Duxford auction in April 1983 to Nalfire Aviation Ltd for £260,000. The consortium that had bought the aircraft was led by former Red Arrows team leader and legendary warbird pilot Ray Hanna. Nalfire eventually became The Old Flying Machine Company (OFMC), and MH434 has been an integral part of this organisation at Duxford for more than 30 years.

MH434's undersides are finished in medium Sea Grey, which was part of the standard day fighter camouflage scheme introduced to Fighter Command by the Air Ministry from 15 August 1941. The only other markings of note are the Type C roundels of 32-inch diameter, which replaced Type A roundels of 50-inch diameter from mid May 1942.

The twin radiators synonymous with Merlin 60/70-series Spitfires are clearly visible in this rear view of MH434. A coolant radiator and the intercooler radiator were under the starboard wing and a second coolant radiator and the oil cooler were situated under the port wing. In this way the engine's cooling system was split, being symmetrical along either side of the engine and airframe.

The enlarged oil tank beneath the engine that gave the PR XI its distinctive 'chin' profile is clearly visible in this view of PL965.

CHAPTER FIVE
SPITFIRES IN BLUE 81

SPITFIRE PR XI PL965

As with the vast majority of the RAF's photo-reconnaissance (PR) Spitfires, PL965 was built in the Aldermaston plant in central Reading, Berkshire. Constructed in the late summer of 1944, the aeroplane was delivered to No 9 MU at Cosford on 2 October and duly prepared for service. Issued to No 1 Pilots' Pool at Benson, in Oxfordshire, on 5 January 1945, the aeroplane was allocated to No 34 Wing six days later as an attrition replacement. PL965 subsequently served with No 16 Squadron from 18 January through to 20 September, undertaking its combat sorties initially from Melsbroek (B 58), in Belgium, and then Eindhoven (B 78), in Holland.

No 16 Squadron was one of three photo-reconnaissance units that were the 'secret eyes' provided by the 2nd Tactical Air Force for the benefit of the 21st Army Group, which was the HQ formation in charge of the British Second Army and the First Canadian Army, as it embarked upon the final assault on Nazi Germany. Over a period of three months, PL965 amassed 75 hours and 25 minutes on operations, with each of its 33 sorties being on average nearly 2.5 hours in duration at an altitude of 4.5 miles above the battlefield. During this period the aeroplane was flown by pilots from Australia, Britain, Belgium, Canada, France and New Zealand. These aviators were a unique breed capable of working for long periods alone, in unpressurised, cramped and freezing conditions, and without the security of either guns or a wingman to watch their tail.

PR Spitfires and Mosquitos were routinely targeted by German fighters, with No 16 Squadron's pilots regularly returning to base with tales of attempted interceptions by Fw 190s and jet-powered Me 262s. Seasoned PR pilot Flight

OPPOSITE TOP The only known wartime photograph of PL965, taken on 26 April 1945 in No 16 Squadron dispersal area at Melbroek. The Spitfire is being marshalled into a parking position, but the lack of visibility over the nose of the aeroplane requires the signals to be relayed to the pilot by two airmen. The aviator in the cockpit may be Flying Officer Jock West, who photographed railway junctions north of Hamburg in this aeroplane on that date according to his logbook. (via Peter R. Arnold)

OPPOSITE Photographic technicians remove a magazine full of exposed film from an F24 14-inch camera mounted for oblique photography in the 'X Type' installation of a Spitfire PR XI. Immediately beneath the oblique camera were the two vertical F52 20- or 36-inch cameras in the 'Universal' installation that shot through the underside of the aeroplane. (via Peter R. Arnold)

ABOVE Cameras fitted in Spitfire XIs were responsible for myriad low-level photographs of this kind of quality from early 1943 through to VE Day. This image reveals the level of destruction achieved by Allied tactical air power when sent against retreating Wehrmacht troop columns during the Battle of the Falaise Pocket in August 1944. In full retreat, the Germans lost thousands of vehicles when they were either destroyed by the enemy or abandoned due to a lack of fuel. (National Archives)

PL965 has been sympathetically refurbished by Peter Teichman since he acquired the aircraft in 2004 for his Hangar 11 Collection at North Weald, returning it to frontline 1944–45 specification. The most significant change occurred in 2010 when the aeroplane's original Merlin 70 engine, overhauled by Eye Tech Engineering, was installed in place of the Packard Merlin 266 that had powered the aeroplane since its return to airworthiness in 1992.

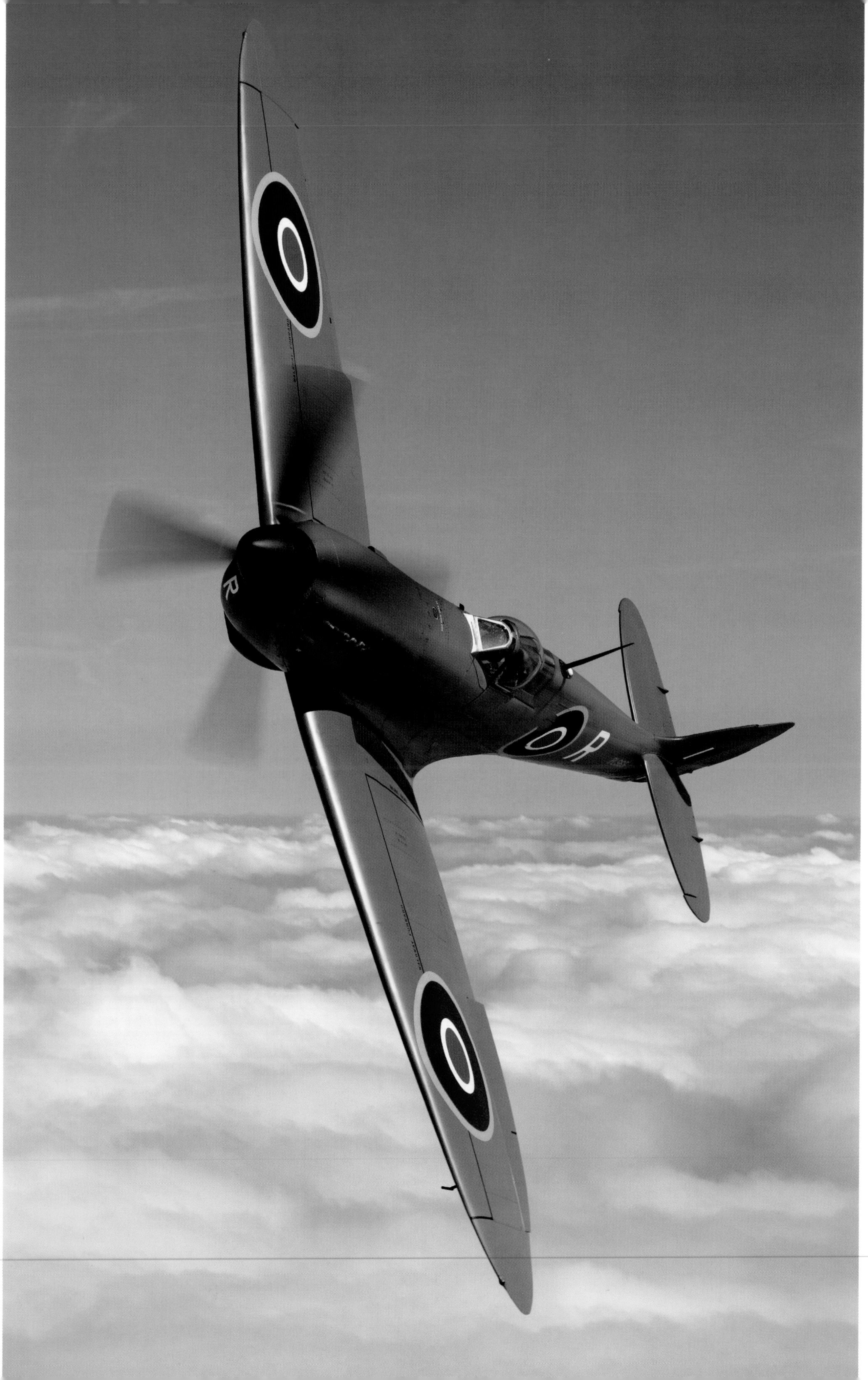

Lieutenant Gordon Bellerby flew five operational sorties in PL965 between 21 March and 28 May 1945:

We did a lot of mapping – northern Germany, Holland and Denmark. In Holland, we were looking for 'Crossbow' [V-weapon] sites. After the Rhine crossing of 24 March there were sorties covering German jet airfields and more mapping. Most trips were at 25,000–26,000 ft just below the condensation trial height in winter in northern Europe. A typical sortie was only two hours long, sometimes less, which was a nice change from four hours-plus trips that I had routinely flown in the Middle East and Italy. German fighters were more interested in bombers than PR aircraft and heavy flak was most unusual. When over Holland, we frequently saw V-2s being fired from around The Hague, and we always took bearings. With three reports of the same site you could get a nice triangulation and then Bomber Command would pay a visit. The USAAF was frankly bad news, and I never lingered in their neighbourhood as their fighter escorts would take off after us.

Flight Lieutenant Bellerby encountered enemy fighters on the very first mission he flew in PL965, on 21 March:

My log book tells me that I was flying a mapping sortie north of Hanover in the Nienburg/Celle area on that date. I made four runs at 26,000 ft, and the sortie lasted 2 hrs 15 min. I have no recollection of the specific target, but I certainly recall the Fw 190 and four Me 262s! The '190 came up just as I finished my runs. I 'went through the gate' [there was a wire 'gate' fitted to the throttle, which the pilot had to break to set the engine to emergency power – the 'gate' acted as an indicator that emergency power had been used and would be replaced by the aircraft's fitter on the ground] and climbed to 30,000 ft, before rapidly leaving the area. There were lots of USAAF aeroplanes around, but I can't recall where they were bombing that day. The '262s scared the hell out of me – after all, four are a bit much!

But somehow they missed seeing me. The pilots must have had their heads inside the cockpit. They crossed beneath my tail at right angles and I kept on going flat for home.

Another pilot to run into enemy fighters in PL965 was Canadian Flight Lieutenant 'Tommy' Thompson:

On the flight in question [5 April 1945] I show in my log book that I was flying at 30,000 ft. I was returning from the Bremen area to Melsbroek. Off my starboard wing I could see two Me 262s headed towards me. I do not recall whether I contacted 'Penman' – our Wing station – but we had had a brief outline their performance, speed etc., and we were told we could not outrun them. Our best form of defence was to attack, as the German pilots were young and inexperienced. While they had been told the blue Spits had no guns, they were not prepared to accept or believe the information received from their Intelligence personnel. With my heart in my mouth I turned into them for the semblance of an attack!

They might have been 2,000 ft below me when I saw them, and at 1,500 ft away I turned on them. They both broke, with the one on my right turning south and diving. I had the advantage and got within 300–400 ft, on his tail. I was very excited, following him down for perhaps a minute. I broke off when I saw cloud cover at somewhere near 20,000 ft. I do not know what happened to the other '262. I know I could have shot the one I tailed down if only I had had guns!

Australian Flying Officer 'Scotty' Caiden flew PL965 on four PR and nine non-operational sorties in 1945. His first flight, on 22 February, ended prematurely when he was forced to abandon an operational sortie due to unserviceable (u/s) engine – this was almost certainly caused by a faulty magneto. He made it back to base with a very rough-running engine, noting in his log book that he was 'down to a nasty low level' by the end of the mission. Technical maladies also afflicted Caiden's final flight in PL965:

I was the last No 16 Squadron pilot to fly the aircraft. The evening before the unit was due to do a flypast and return to England and disbandment [on 17 September 1945], '965 became temperamental and ground-staff advised me that it was u/s and I would not be able to leave with the rest of the squadron. I hung around for a couple of days whilst ground-staff laboured mightily, eventually declaring '965 airworthy. Even then it seemed the old war-horse was reluctant to leave the scene of its gallant exploits.

Airborne, the radio packed up – frightful weather – so I returned to Eindhoven. Another attempt was made the next day. Same story, and had to creep into Knoke. Next day I kicked '965 smartly on one of the oleos. 'This is it, old boy' – and off we went, up to 38,000 ft over all the weather and presto, made it! I was quite upset to leave my Spitfire all alone at Dunsfold, looking very forlorn.

By 11 October 1945 PL965 was with No 151 Repair Unit at Wevelgem, near Brussels, and it subsequently became one of eight Spitfires purchased by the RNAF on 8 July 1947 exclusively for technical training. The aeroplane was taken on charge by the School of Technical Training at Deelan on 6 August, being used primarily for instruction in engine running. Eventually retired in 1952, PL965 was resurrected using parts from three other Spitfires in 1955 and put on display as a Mk IX outside the Sergeants' Mess at Deelan. It remained here until moved to the National War and Resistance Museum at Overloon on 22 November 1960.

Despite being refurbished twice over the next 26 years, PL965 steadily deteriorated at the open air museum at Overloon until it was swapped for an ex-IAF Spitfire XIV in March 1987. The latter machine was supplied by Nick Grace and Chris Horsley, who in turn hoped to restore PL965 to airworthiness. The Medway Aircraft Preservation Society (MAPS) at Rochester Airport, in Kent, was given the job of refurbishing the aeroplane's fuselage, and good progress was made up until the untimely death of Nick Grace in a car accident in October 1988. Full ownership then passed to Chris Horsley, who in turn made the decision to commission MAPS to complete the entire restoration. PL965 eventually returned to the air, from Rochester, on 23 December 1992. The Spitfire duly moved to Duxford in February of the following year, where it was operated by OFMC whilst owned by Chris Horsley.

In March 1997 the aeroplane was sold to The Real Aeroplane Company, based at Breighton in Yorkshire, who in turn shipped it to Florida in September 2001. The Spitfire remained in the USA until May 2004, having performed at a number of airshows in and around Florida. Three months after its return to the UK PL965 was acquired by its current owner, Peter Teichman, for his Hangar 11 Collection based at North Weald, in Essex. In 2009–10 the aircraft was the subject of a major overhaul, during which the Spitfire's original Merlin 70 engine (rebuilt by Maurice Hammond of Eye Tech Engineering) was reinstalled in place of the Packard Merlin 266 that had powered the aeroplane since its return to airworthiness in 1992.

Immediately below the fuselage roundel are the camera ports – covered by quarter-inch plate glass – for the Spitfire PR XI's vertical 'Universal' installation, which is situated between the rear fuselage frames 13, 14 and 15. Two vertical cameras ('fanned' F8 20-inch, which was later replaced by the F52 20- or 36-inch camera, or 'fanned' F24 14-inch) could be installed. The vertical cameras were principally used for surveillance, mapping and bomb damage assessment from medium to high altitude. They were normally matched and vertically 'fanned' to port and starboard so that two overlapping photographs could be taken simultaneously.

SPITFIRE PR XIX PS853

Although ordered from Vickers Armstrongs (Supermarine) on 17 July 1943 as one of 200 HF VIIIs, PS853 was built as a PR XIX when the order was revised to cover the construction of 121 Spitefuls – the majority of which were cancelled – and 79 photo-reconnaissance Spitfires. According to official documentation, the aeroplane was completed by the Southampton works on 5 September 1944, although this does not tally up with delivery dates of aircraft built within this range of serials. It is more likely that PS853 was constructed in November or December of that year, the aeroplane also being described in company paperwork as a 'Production Prototype' used to trial an unspecified modification to the PR XIX.

PS853 was sent to the Central Photographic Reconnaissance Unit at Benson on 13 January 1945, from where it was transferred to No 16 Squadron of No 34 Wing at B 58 Melsbroek, in Belgium, six weeks later. Receiving its first three PR XIXs on 17 March (PS853 was coded 'C' by the unit, possibly indicating that it was the third example delivered to B 58), No 16 Squadron had five on charge by the 27th. These aircraft were flown alongside the Spitfire PR XIs that had served

with the unit since August 1943, including PL965 featured earlier in this book. Pilots on the squadron undertook a five-hour conversion course onto the PR XIX, after which they were cleared from operational missions.

PS853's first such sortie took place on 2 April 1945 from B 77 Gilze-Rijen, in Holland, when Flight Lieutenant Eric Martin (who also flew PL965 operationally that same month) was ordered to scramble and make several runs over The Hague. This area was being used by mobile V-2 launchers, and No 16 Squadron had been tasked with locating the vengeance weapons for attack by 2nd TAF fighter-bombers. Martin and PS853 made similar flights over this area during 3–4 April too, and he also flew a Meteorological Reconnaissance mission over the North Sea on the latter date after completing his coverage of Holland. No 16 Squadron moved to B 78 Eindhoven on 10 April, and it continued to operate from here through to VE Day.

On 19 September No 16 Squadron disbanded and then reformed two days later at B 116 Celle, in Germany, when No 268 Squadron was renumbered. PS853 remained on strength with the unit throughout this period, before eventually returning

to the UK in March 1946 and being passed on to No 29 MU at High Ercall the following month. It suffered a Category B flying accident on 17 January 1949, and the aeroplane had to be returned to the manufacturer for repairs. After more than a year in Supermarine's South Marston plant, PS853 was flown to No 6 MU at Brize Norton on 30 March 1950. Transferred to No 9 MU at Cosford on

13 July that same year, the aeroplane was eventually selected by No 41 Group (Maintenance Command) on 10 March 1952 for allocation to the Short Brothers & Harland-operated Temperature and Humidity (THUM) Flight at Woodvale, in Lancashire. Flown to No 32 MU at St Athan, in Wales, on 17 April 1952, the aeroplane was modified here for its new role.

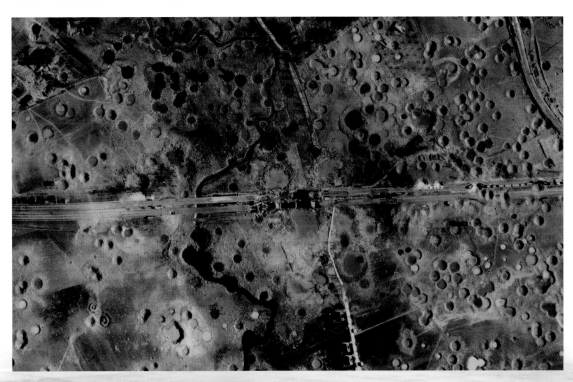

BELOW PS853 served with Temperature and Humidity (THUM) flight for more than five years, completing 815 weather reconnaissance sorties during this period – including the last flight by a Spitfire serving the RAF in an operational capacity (on 9 June 1957). It is seen here taxiing across the apron at Speke airport, in Liverpool, in April 1957. Speke acted as the reception point for the weather data collected during THUM flights. (Jennifer Gradidge via Peter R. Arnold)

THUM Flight was a dedicated weather reconnaissance unit, run under contract, to give flyers, both military and civilian, up-to-date weather details for the UK. In order to perform this task, PS853 was one of eight PR XIXs – and a solitary Spitfire F 24 – given a 'Special Fitting' at St Athan, which consisted of a barometer and data recording gear stowed in the bay previously occupied by cameras. Author Ken Ellis described a typical THUM Flight sortie in his article 'Rule of THUM', published in the July 2007 issue of *FlyPast* magazine:

> Climb, while constantly monitoring the instruments and engine state. Maintain position during a spiral around a point north of Worcester. Level off, trim. Take readings, note weather conditions, cloud type and check the dials again. Throttle forward, climb again and repeat at intervals until 30,000 ft is reached. Descend and set course for Liverpool.
>
> This was exacting, repetitious flying. Frequently, it was conducted in ten-tenths cloud, with eyes glued to the turn-and-bank indicators, broken by frequent glimpses at the airspeed, vertical speed, temperatures and pressures, compass and altimeter. Sweating and tired, at least the flight back allowed the pilot to luxuriate in the rewards of this intensive flying. Here was a chance to revel in the last-serving Supermarine Spitfires in the RAF, the high-performing PR 19.
>
> And all of this to give flyers, military and civilian, weather details for the UK. The Spitfires were sent out daily at 0800 hrs to take regular readings of temperatures and humidity from 1,500 ft up to 30,000 ft.

A veteran of combat in Malaya in the Spitfire XVIII, as well as a MiG-killer when on exchange with the USAF during the Korean War, Wing Commander Nicholls (far right) was eminently qualified to fly PS853 against the Lightning. He also had experience of the English Electric fighter, having been the RAF's Liaison Officer during test-flying of the F 3 variant immediately prior to being posted to the Air Fighting Development Squadron. (via Peter R. Arnold)

PS853 served with the flight until it was finally retired in 1957, having completed the last of its 815 THUM flights on 9 June. The three remaining Woodvale Spitfire XIXs joined the newly established Historic Aircraft Flight at Biggin Hill in July of that year, PS853 being flown from Duxford to the famous fighter station by Group Captain 'Johnnie' Johnson. The flight moved to North Weald, in Essex, on 1 March the following year, although its place with the unit was taken by one of three Spitfire LF XVIEs that had been taken on charge.

Flown to the Central Fighter Establishment (CFE) at West Raynham, in Norfolk, on 14 April 1958 to be used as a gate guardian, it was struck off charge on 1 May but kept in airworthy condition and flown on at least 12 occasions between 17 May 1958 and 16 November 1960. Fully overhauled by No 19 MU at St Athan in 1961, PS853 was brought back on charge by the CFE in November 1962 – the unit had moved to Binbrook, in North Yorkshire, the previous month. The aeroplane was officially part of the CFE Communications Flight.

LEFT Wing Commander John Nicholls, Officer Commanding the Air Fighting Development Squadron within the Central Fighter Establishment, flew PS853 in a series of trial combat missions against Lightnings from Binbrook in 1963. Photographed from the base control tower, the two fighter types perform a low-level pass along the flightline at the North Yorkshire airfield. (via Peter R. Arnold)

BOTTOM PS853 serves as the backdrop at the official establishment of the RAF's Historic Aircraft Flight at Biggin Hill on 11 July 1957, the aeroplane having been flown from Duxford to the famous fighter station by ranking Spitfire ace Group Captain 'Johnnie' Johnson. He can be seen standing immediately behind Air Marshal Sir Thomas Pike, Air Officer Commanding RAF Fighter Command, who is addressing the assembled crowd. The remaining two pilots in flying overalls are, at far left, Wing Commander Peter Thompson (a Battle of Britain veteran and then station commander of Biggin Hill) and fellow Spitfire ace Group Captain Jamie Rankin. Thompson, who played a key role in setting up the Historic Aircraft Flight, and Rankin had flown two other ex-THUM Flight PR XIXs (PM631 and PS915, which are both still with the Battle of Britain Memorial Flight) from Duxford to Biggin Hill. (via Peter R. Arnold)

During 1963 the Officer Commanding the Air Fighting Development Squadron within the CFE, Wing Commander John Nicholls, flew PS853 in a series of trial flights against Lightnings from Binbrook. A veteran of combat in Malaya in the Spitfire XVIII, as well as a MiG killer when on exchange with the USAF during the Korean War, he described the reason behind these unusual sorties, and the flights themselves, in Alfred Price's *Spitfire At War* book, published in 1974:

This was at the time of the Indonesian confrontation and, since the Indonesian Air Force operated a large number of P-51 Mustang fighters, we were very interested in discovering how best a Lightning might engage such an aircraft. In the RAF we did not have any Mustangs, but at Binbrook we did have our Spitfire with a performance that was, in many respects, similar. Thus it came about that our Spitfire came to be involved in a short battle trial pitted against a fighter that was her successor by three generations.

Of course, from the start we knew that the Lightning could overtake the Spitfire by nearly 1,000 mph – there was no need to run a trial to prove that. But we did find that the piston-engined fighter presented a very poor target to infra-red homing missiles, especially from the rear aspect. And, since the Lightning would therefore very likely have to follow up its missile pass with a gun attack, a high overtaking speed would have made accurate firing very difficult. On the other hand, if the Lightning pilot slowed down too much he could end up playing the slower and more manoeuvrable fighter's dogfighting game and lose. None of this was new – we had learned the same thing during trials between the Lightning and the Hunter. Another problem was that if the Spitfire pilot had sufficient warning of the attack he could spin around to meet it head-on – and thus present the most difficult target of all.

In the end we evolved a type of attack that was the antitheses of all I had learned from my own operational experience of fighters-versus-fighters combat over Korea. Instead of trying to get above the enemy and diving on him to attack, we found it best to use the Lightning's very high power-to-weight ratio to make a climbing attack from behind and below. From that angle the field-of-view from the Spitfire was poor, there was a good chance of achieving surprise and the infra-red source gave the best chance for missile acquisition. If the Lightning pilot did not acquire the target or bring his guns to bear on his first pass he could continue his steep climb – which the Spitfire could not possibly follow – and when out of range he could dive and repeat the process. Using such tactics, we felt that in the end a competent Lightning pilot could almost always get the better of an equally competent Spitfire (or Mustang) pilot.

Almost certainly that trial at Binbrook was the final operational act carried out in earnest in the Spitfire's long career.

On 14 April 1964 PS853 joined the BBMF at Coltishall, in Norfolk, and four years later it participated in the filming of *The Battle of Britain*. Overhauled at Kemble, in Gloucestershire, in 1971, the aeroplane had its original Griffon 66 engine replaced with an ex-Shackleton Griffon RG30 during 1985–86 – this work was carried out by both BBMF and Rolls-Royce engineers. In 1994 the decision was made to sell PS853 so as to secure funds for the rebuilding of Hurricane II LF363, which had been all but destroyed in a forced landing and fire at Wittering, in Cambridgeshire, in September 1991. On 15 February 1995 the aeroplane was sold to Euan English for a reported £345,000 and delivered to North Weald 48 hours later. English was killed in a Harvard crash on 4 March that same year, and the Spitfire was sold to Rolls-Royce plc on 19 September 1996 as a replacement for Mk XIV RM689, which had been badly damaged in a fatal crash on 29 June 1992. PS853 has remained in its ownership ever since, being assigned to the company's Corporate Heritage Department and, since 2008, permanently based at East Midlands Airport.

Like the Spitfire PR XI, the PR XIX was fitted with a one-piece wraparound windscreen in place of the bullet-proof version found on armed variants of the aircraft. The aeroplane was also built with PR XI wings, which had been modified to allow more fuel tanks to be between the spars just outboard of the wheel bays in the space occupied by wing cameras in the early aircraft.

OPPOSITE The camera installation in the PR XIX was broadly similar to that found in the PR XI, with a 'Universal' fitting provided for either two 'fanned' or a single F52 36-inch vertical camera, two 'fanned' F52 20-inch vertical or two 'fanned' F24 14-inch vertical cameras and one F24 14-inch or eight-inch oblique. The two vertical camera ports, covered by quarter-inch plate glass, are visible immediately below the fuselage roundel.

RIGHT Between September 2010 and October 2012 PS853 had its first major overhaul some 65 years after entering service with the RAF, the work being carried out by the Aircraft Restoration Company at Duxford. 'It's a lovely aeroplane, and in a display scenario you certainly appreciate having more power', explained Phill O'Dell, Chief Pilot at Rolls-Royce plc – PS853 is maintained by the company's Corporate Heritage Department. 'We fly any Spitfire well within its particular performance envelope, but you have to work a bit harder in a "baby" [Mk Is, IIs, and Vs] to maintain the required energy.'

'This Spitfire is very much more powerful than the Merlin-engined versions', noted Phill O'Dell, 'but if you treat it with respect and do everything that you do progressively, then it is an absolute beauty. If you slam full power on, it will jump sideways, so you don't do that, but if you slowly apply power and use the rudder to compensate, then she's a pussycat.'

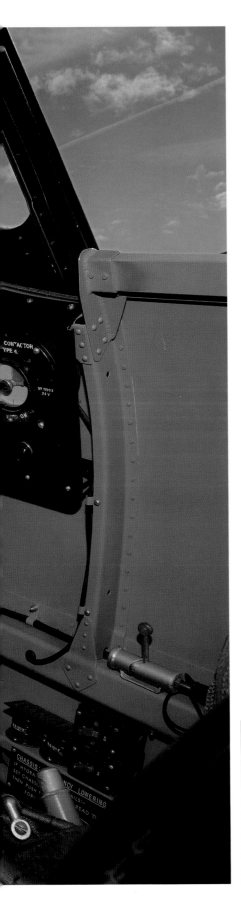

CHAPTER SIX

PACKARD MERLIN SPITFIRE

LF XVIE RW382

Originally ordered from Castle Bromwich on 20 January 1944 as part of an order for 700 Spitfire 21s that was subsequently cancelled in August 1944, RW382 was finally built in June–July 1945 when the initial order was partially reinstated to cover the construction of 40 Mk IXs. In a final twist, the aircraft was actually completed as a low-back LF XVIE, powered by a Packard Merlin 266 engine. Delivered to No 6 MU at Brize Norton on 20 July, the fighter remained in storage until issued to the Royal Auxiliary Air Force's No 604 'County of Middlesex' Squadron on 1 April 1947. The unit was then based at Hendon, although it moved to North Weald on 28 March 1949 when it was re-designated a training unit. RW382 remained with the squadron until 14 April 1950, when it was replaced by a Vampire F 3 as No 604 Squadron embraced the jet age. The fighter was flown to No 33 MU at Lyneham and placed in storage.

RW382 joined No 3 Civilian Anti-Aircraft Co-operation Unit at Exeter, in Devon, on 11 June 1951, transferring to the Control and Reporting School at Middle Wallop, in Hampshire, on 17 October that same year. The fighter was eventually retired on 14 July 1953 when it was flown to No 45 MU at Kinloss, in Scotland, moving to No 29 MU at High Ercall, in Shropshire, two weeks later. Following a year in storage, RW382 was issued to No 609 Squadron at Church Fenton, in North Yorkshire, as an instructional airframe on 28 November 1955. In mid 1959 the fighter took up gate guardian duties at Leconfield, in Yorkshire, where it remained until transported to Henlow, in Bedfordshire,

The Spitfire Company Ltd restored the cockpit of RW382 to late war specification, choosing to fit a conventional GM 2 reflector gunsight rather than a GGS Mk II gyro gunsight – an item that would have been fitted in LF XVIEs by this late stage of the conflict, but one that is rarely seen in restored Spitfires.

LEFT Built too late to see active service in World War 2, RW382 spent almost two years in storage until finally issued to the Royal Auxiliary Air Force's No 604 'County of Middlesex' Squadron on 1 April 1947. The aeroplane is seen here, in its original factory-applied camouflage, at the unit's Hendon home shortly after its assignment to No 604 Squadron. (F. K. Griffiths via Peter R. Arnold)

RIGHT During RW382's recent restoration to airworthiness, the aeroplane was converted into a highback LF XVIE and marked up as a No 322 'Dutch' Squadron aircraft. The unit had flown Spitfires from Biggin Hill on 'Ramrods' and armed reconnaissance sweeps across the North Sea between 31 October 1944 and 3 January 1945. On the latter date it moved to B 79 Woensdrecht, in Holland, to join No 132 Wing of the 2nd Tactical Air Force. Flying mainly ground support sorties through to war's end, No 322 Squadron subsequently operated from four airfields on the continent as it kept pace with Allied troops advancing into northwest Europe. The unit's hardworking groundcrews had to carry out routine servicing in the open, as seen here, because most airfields boasted little in the way of facilities – the latter had either been bombed out by the Allies prior to the airfields' capture or blown up by the retreating Germans. (via Chris Thomas)

OPPOSITE No 604 Squadron moved to North Weald in March 1949, by which time the unit had ditched the wartime camouflage for a more modern overall aluminium finish. Maintained in immaculate condition, RW382 was photographed during North Weald's Battle of Britain at Home open day in September 1949. Two months later No 604 Squadron commenced its conversion to Vampire F 3s, although RW382 remained with the unit until mid April 1950. (John D. Rawlings via Peter R. Arnold)

on 24 February 1967 for restoration to taxiing condition for use as set-dressing in *The Battle of Britain* film. Returned to Leconfield on 5 December 1969, the aeroplane was moved to Uxbridge and mounted on a pole near the main gate.

RW382 was eventually moved to the Clive Denney/Historic Flying Ltd (HFL) workshop at Braintree, in Essex, in August 1988 for restoration to airworthiness as part of a deal involving a number of gate guard Spitfires, glass-fibre replacement 'Spitfires' and a P-40 and a Bristol Beaufort. The latter two aircraft were owned by David Tallichet's Military Aircraft Restoration Corporation, and were destined for the RAF Museum in a swap for a fully restored RW382. The airframe was moved to HFL's new workshop at Audley End, in Essex, for a rebuild, while its Merlin 266 was overhauled by Vintage V-12s in California. The aeroplane made its first post-restoration flight on 3 July 1991, and despite being owned by David Tallichet, RW382 remained in the UK until it was sold to Bernie Jackson and shipped to the USA in early 1995. Jackson's nephew Tom (an ex-Canadian Armed Forces Hornet pilot) was killed when RW382 struck high ground near Blue Canyon, in

California on 3 June 1998. He had departed Chino in the fighter bound for Minden, Nevada, but had run into bad weather en route and crashed 30 minutes into the flight.

The wreckage of RW382 was recovered and delivered to Airframe Assemblies in Sandown on 22 August 2001. Eventually bought by Pemberton-Billing LLP in July 2008, the fighter commenced its second restoration to airworthiness shortly thereafter. The fuselage, now in high back configuration, was rebuilt at Airframe Assemblies and then moved to Peter Monk's workshop at Biggin Hill in February 2011 for fitting out and painting by The Spitfire Company Ltd. Fitted with a refurbished Merlin 66, the aeroplane successfully completed its first flight after its second restoration on 18 September 2013.

During the rebuild, RW382 was marked in the colours of No 322 'Dutch' Squadron, which flew Spitfires (initially LF IXEs and then LF XVIEs) from Biggin Hill on 'Ramrods' and armed reconnaissance sweeps across the North Sea between 31 October 1944 and 3 January 1945. On the latter date the unit moved to B 79 Woensdrecht, in Holland, to join No 132 Wing of the 2nd Tactical Air Force.

Inspired by No 322 Squadron's
two-month spell at 'Biggin on the
bump', The Spitfire Company Ltd
applied an accurate colour scheme
to RW382 as worn by the Dutch
unit's Spitfire LF IXEs and LF XVIEs
prior to their move to the
continent. As the black and white
photograph of the No 322
Squadron aeroplane in this chapter
clearly shows, the unit sprayed out
the Sky fuselage band with
camouflage paint and switched to
black propeller spinners in an effort
to make its Spitfires less
conspicuous on airfields close to
the frontline. Finally, the upper wing
roundels changed from two-colour
Type Bs to 32-inch Type Cs,
complete with a white inner ring
and yellow outline – identical, in
fact, to the roundels on the
underside of the wing.

RW382's orange triangle marking, as applied by Dutch-manned squadrons to their aircraft whilst serving with the RAF in World War 2, stands out against the aeroplane's otherwise standard day fighter camouflage scheme. The equal-sided orange triangle, outlined in black, was adopted by the Royal Netherlands Air Force as its national marking from October 1939. The symbol was seen on all five marks of Spitfire flown by No 322 Squadron following its formation in June 1943 (with the renumbering of No 167 Squadron).

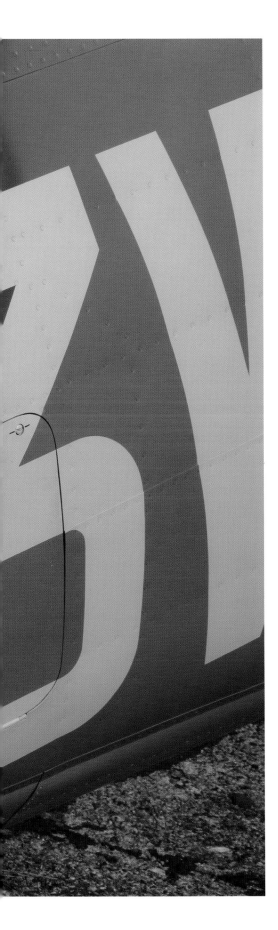

The quality of the paintwork that has been applied to RW382 is plain to see in this close-up of the rear fuselage. The DTD 517 S stencilling appeared on Spitfires from 1943 when matt-pigmented synthetic resin primer and finish replaced DTD 308 cellulose paint. DTD 517 was selected for application to Spitfires in place of DTD 308 because it was easier to apply and gave an aerodynamically smooth finish. The paint also proved to be more durable, and its manufacture did not involve the use of nitro-cellulose, which was also in high demand in the manufacturing process for explosives. The W/T (wireless transmitter) stencil above DTD 517 S was applied as a form of inspection stamp to show that the aircraft's earthing had been tested. A short circuit, caused by precipitation for example, could cause sparking that in turn adversely affected the aeroplane's radio reception.

Flying mainly ground support sorties through to war's end, No 322 Squadron subsequently operated from four airfields on the continent as it kept pace with Allied troops advancing into northwest Europe.

The unit only saw German aircraft twice during this period when it carried out two separate strafing attacks on airfields (one of which was Wittmundhafen, identified as 'Ardorf' by the pilot involved) northwest of Bremen on 25 April. A Ju 188 was destroyed and two Bf 109s damaged, with Flight Lieutenant Gordon Braidwood being the most successful pilot on these missions. Posted to the unit as a flight commander just two days earlier, his Personal Combat Report for the morning sortie, flown between 0850 hrs and 1005 hrs from B 106 Twente, in Holland, read as follows:

I took off on an Armed Recce for transport in Aurich A area, and, while flying at 5,000 ft, saw a Me 109 parked in a field. I made one attack from tail to nose with cannon and machine gun fire, followed by my No 2. As there was no flak I made a second attack, also followed by my No 2. Many strikes were seen on the enemy aircraft and it was smoking considerably but not burning when we left.

Flight Lieutenant Braidwood took off again at 1205 hrs in search of more targets, as his second Personal Combat Report details:

A section of two [Spitfires] set out [from B 106 Twente] with 45-gallon overload [tanks] and 2 X 250 lb MC .025-sec wing bombs. My No 2 turned back at Meppen with engine trouble and I went alone. I approached Ardorf airfield from the south at 8,000 ft, jettisoned overload [tanks] and dived vertically to 2,000 ft on two Ju 188s parked on the southwest side of the airfield. One bomb was direct hit on the southernmost aircraft and the other fell just behind the second one. I orbited and photographed the bomb bursts from 2,000 ft, and also strafed. Both aircraft were obscured with smoke and debris from the bomb bursts.

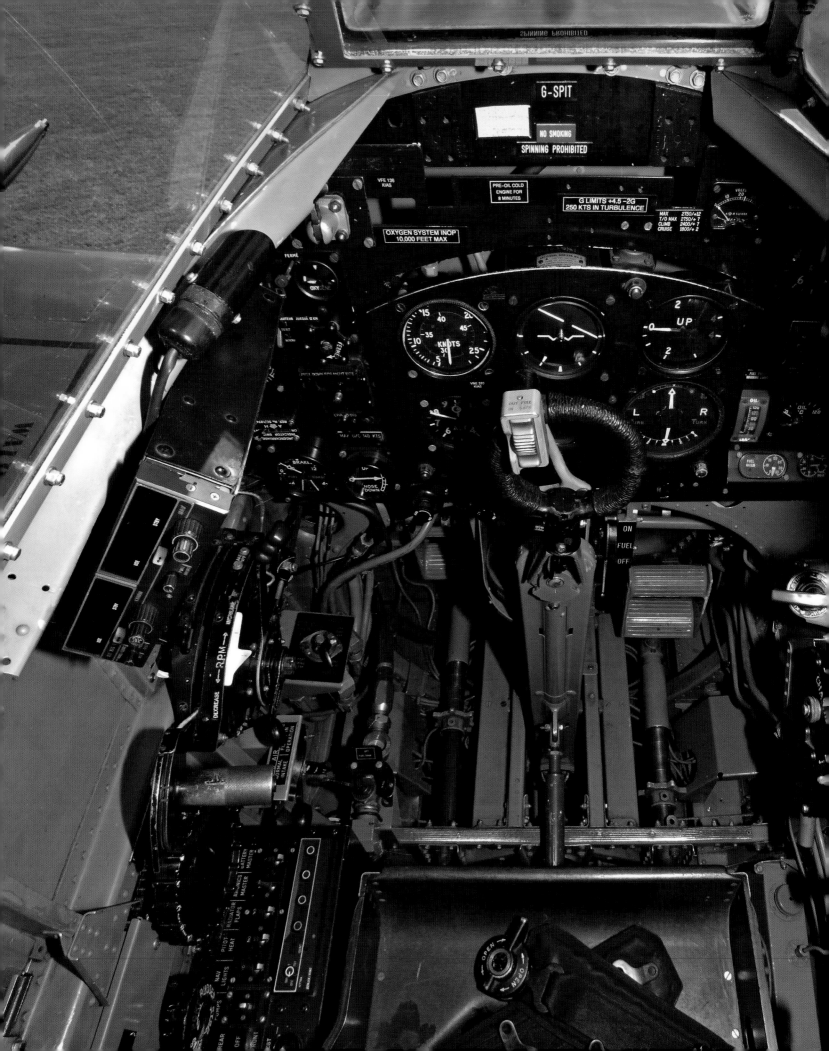

The tight confines of the Spitfire FR XIVE's cockpit. Throughout the 'Joker' routine, Stephen Grey pulled an almost continuous 4–5 G in this aeroplane, which was only relieved by the occasional vertical climb to allow him to keep a visual check on the progress of the oncoming 'Balbo'.

CHAPTER SEVEN

GRIFFON SPITFIRES

SPITFIRE FR XIV MV293

Built as part of a mixed batch of 700 Mk VIIIs and XIVs that formed the second order for the Mk VIII placed with Supermarine Aviation (Vickers) Ltd on 27 July 1942, MV293 was assembled at Keevil, in Wiltshire in July 1944. The latter site was just one of a number of dispersed locations in southern England that were used for Spitfire assembly during this late war period, aircraft from this order also being built in Southampton, Eastleigh, Aldermaston and Chattis Hill, in Hampshire. It appears that MV293 was possibly one of several Mk XIVs used as production prototypes for aileron modifications from 25 July 1944, the Griffon-engined Spitfire initially being afflicted by aileron issues.

MV293 was eventually delivered to No 33 MU at Lyneham on 27 February 1945 and stored after it was taken on charge on 1 March. The fighter was despatched to No 215 MU at Dumfries, in Scotland, on 20 August for packing and, four days later, it arrived at Birkenhead ready for shipment to India. MV293 was duly loaded onboard the SS *Dee Bank*, which sailed for Karachi on 6 September. The fighter reached its destination on 14 October and was received by Air Command South East Asia (ACSEA) nine days later. Loaned to No 8 Squadron of the Royal Indian Air Force (RIAF), MV293 was permanently transferred to the IAF on 29/31 December 1947. By then No 8 Squadron, based at Kolar, in southern India, had converted to the Tempest II and the Spitfire was declared surplus to requirements. It is likely that the aircraft was one of a number of redundant fighters transported the short distance from Kolar to the IAF's Technical College at Jallahali, in Bangalore.

MV293 was one of a number of Spitfires that the Indian government offered for sale by tender to foreign customers in

TOP Although built in Wiltshire, MV293 was destined never to serve with the RAF either in the UK or abroad. Shipped to Karachi in September 1945 and eventually loaned to No 8 Squadron of the Royal Indian Air Force (RIAF), MV293 was permanently transferred to the IAF on 29/31 December 1947. Still wearing ACSEA's Temperate Land Scheme (Dark Green and Dark Earth over Medium Sea Grey under-surfaces) and RAF codes and identification bands in white, but with IAF roundels and fin flashes in saffron, white and green, MV293 was photographed possibly at Kolar, in southern India, during its brief time with No 8 Squadron. (via Peter R. Arnold)

ABOVE During the final stages of its restoration to airworthiness in 1992, MV293 was marked up in an aluminium scheme inspired by No 2 Squadron Spitfire FR XIVEs based in Germany post-war. However, in 2000, the aeroplane was repainted in the colours worn by MV268 during the final months of World War 2 in Europe. The latter was one of at least two Griffon-engined Spitfires assigned to Group Captain J. E. 'Johnnie' Johnson during his time as CO of No 125 Wing. This rare photograph of the aeroplane was taken in April 1945, possibly at B 78 Eindhoven. (via Andy Thomas)

the mid 1970s, the remains of the aeroplane being acquired by British warbird pioneer Doug Arnold. It arrived in England on 26 May 1978, being delivered to Blackbushe, in Hampshire. Dick Melton commenced restoration work on the fighter at this location, and this was continued by Pete Rushen at Ruskington, in Lincolnsire, after the Spitfire was acquired by The Fighter Collection (TFC) in late 1985. The aircraft was subsequently transferred to Duxford when Rushen became TFC's Chief Engineer, MV293 making its first post-restoration flight on 14 August 1992. The fighter was initially flown in an overall silver scheme as worn by No 2 Squadron Spitfire FR XIVs based in West Germany in the late 1940s. In 2000, it was repainted as MV268, which was the personal aircraft of Group Captain J. E. 'Johnnie' Johnson during his time as CO of No 125 Wing in the final weeks of the war in Europe.

The leading RAF ace in northwest Europe with 34 and seven shared victories (all claimed in Spitfires), Johnson joined No 125 Wing at B 78 Eindhoven, in Holland, on 6 April 1945 and led it on the final sweeps over enemy-held territory. Although he failed to make any claims in Griffon-engined Spitfires, Johnson witnessed a number of victories scored by pilots under his command, including fellow ace, Wing Commander George Keefer. The Wing was particularly busy on 18 April when Keefer led it to Parchim, where the Spitfire XIV pilots spotted a group of 11 Bf 109s preparing to take off. A series of strafing attacks were immediately carried out, during which Keefer personally claimed five of the Messerschmitt fighters destroyed. The action had been witnessed by Group Captain 'Johnnie' Johnson:

RIGHT Group Captain 'Johnnie' Johnson, the leading RAF ace in northwest Europe, joined No 125 Wing at B 78 Eindhoven on 6 April 1945. (via Andy Thomas)

BELOW Group Captain 'Johnnie' Johnson was also assigned FR XIV MV257, which bore much smaller 'JEJ' code letters just forward of the cockpit on either side of the fuselage. This aircraft replaced MV268 shortly after VE Day, and was flown by Johnson when he led No 125 Wing in a celebratory flypast over Copenhagen from its base at nearby Kastrup in June 1945. This was the last Spitfire to bear Johnson's initials. (via Chris Thomas)

MV293, masquerading as MV268, is flown over agricultural land near its Duxford home by Stephen Grey of The Fighter Collection. Stephen put the aircraft through its paces during the Flying Legends airshow weekend in July 2003 when he used it to perform the high-energy, high-G 'Joker' routine that has traditionally kept the crowd entertained during the forming up of 30-plus piston-engined fighters and bombers for the event's unique 'Balbo' finale.

I saw Wing Commander Keefer and Flying Officer Trevorrow [who was credited with six Bf 109s destroyed] make their attack on the 11 '109s. Four were hit and started to burn. I then orbited the aerodrome at 6,000 ft and saw several large explosions as the remainder of the tightly packed formations caught fire. All 11 were completely burned out, and as we passed the aerodrome 20 minutes later a dense pall of smoke reached 10,000 ft.

Five days later No 125 Wing, again led by Group Captain 'Johnnie' Johnson, flew a historic sweep over Berlin in his F XIV, wearing the code 'JEJ', where the Spitfire pilots met around 100 Soviet Yak-9 fighters:

I led the wing on the Berlin show at the first opportunity. For this epic occasion our first team took to the air. George [Keefer, who was the Wing Leader] led a squadron and [Australian ace] Tony Gaze flew with me again – the first time since we had flown together in Bader's Wing [in 1941]. We swept to Berlin at a couple of thousand feet above the ground, over a changing sunlit countryside of desolate heathland, small lakes and large forests, with the empty, double ribbon of the autobahn lying close on our starboard side.

We shall not easily forget our first sight of Berlin. Thick cloud covered the capital and forced us down to a lower level. The roads to the west were filled with a mad of refugees fleeing the city. We pressed over the wooded suburbs, and Berlin sprawled below us with gaping holes here and there. It was burning in a dozen different places. The Russian artillery was hard at it – as we flew towards the east we saw the flashes of their guns and the debris thrown up from the shells. Russian tanks and armour rumbled into the city from the east. Tony said;

'Fifty-plus at at "two o'clock", Greycap! Same level. More behind.'

'Are they Huns Tony?' I asked, as I focused my eyes on the gaggle.

'Don't look like Huns to me, Greycap', replied Tony. 'Probably Russians'.

'All right chaps', I said. 'Stick together. Don't make a move'. And to myself I thought, 'I'm for it if this mix-up gets out of hand!'

The Yaks began a slow turn which would bring them behind our Spitfires. I could not allow this, and I swung the Wing to starboard and turned over the top of the Yaks. They numbered about 100 all told.

'More above us', calmly reported Tony.

'Tighten it up', I ordered. 'Don't break formation'.

We circled each other for a couple of turns. Both sides were cautious and suspicious. I narrowed the gap between us as much as I dared. When I was opposite the Russian leader I rocked my wings and watched for him to do the same. He paid no regard, but soon after he straightened out of his turn and led his ragged collection back to the east.

We watched them fly away. There seemed to be no pattern or discipline to their flying. The leader was in front and the pack followed behind, rising and falling, with the gaggle continually changing shape. They reminded me of a great wheeling, tumbling pack of starlings which one sometimes sees on a winter day in England. They quartered the ground like buzzards, and every few moments a handful broke away from the pack, circled leisurely and then attacked something in the desert of brick and rubble. In this fashion they worked over the dying city.

We were not allowed to fly over Berlin again, and perhaps it was just as well, for there could easily have been an unfortunate clash between the Russians and ourselves, especially during bad weather with poor visibility. A high-level decision was made to halt our armies on the Elbe, and once again we patrolled the area between Celle and the Baltic coast.

We found a lot of Huns during the latter half of April. We took off before first light to get at them, and the last patrols landed on the flare path. We destroyed fighters, bombers, transports, Stuka dive-bombers, those once dreaded peregrines of the *Blitzkrieg*, trainers and a bunch of seaplanes we found floating on a lake. We could not catch the jets in the air, but we knew they were operating from Lübeck, on the Baltic coast. We paid special attention to this airfield, shooting them down when they took off or came in to land. Some of the enemy leaders showed flashes of their old brilliance, but the rank and file were poor stuff.

Culmhead Wing leader, and ace, Wing Commander Pete Brothers was a great proponent of the Spitfire XIV, noting, 'It was a truly impressive machine...' (via John Dibbs)

'Johnnie' Johnson exclusively flew Spitfires in the frontline, claiming the vast majority of his victories in the Mk IX. He was not a great fan of the Mk XIV, however, commenting after his first flight in one that it was 'a nice, fast flying machine, but it's not a Spitfire anymore'. Indeed, Johnson went as far as to say that the 'Griffon-engined fighter was so different it should have had another name. The Spitfire XIV was designed as a high-altitude fighter, but its powerful engine produced a lot of torque, which meant that the aeroplane needed constant trimming, especially when manoeuvring. I preferred the Mk IX – the best of them all'.

This was not a view shared by Jeffrey Quill, who stated in his autobiography that in his opinion the 'Mk XIV turned out to be the best of all the fighter variants of the Spitfire. It fully justified the faith of those who from the early days in 1939 had been convinced that the Griffon engine would eventually see the Spitfire into new lease of life. I flew the first production Mk XIV, RB140, in October 1943.

It was a splendid and potent aeroplane. It was powerful and it performed magnificently'.

Culmhead Wing leader, and ace, Wing Commander Pete Brothers was also a proponent of the Spitfire XIV, and he too had seen plenty of combat in various marks of the fighter since switching from the Hurricane shortly after the Battle of Britain:

My Wing comprised two squadrons equipped with Spitfire F VIIs and a solitary unit with the Mk XIV. Although the Mk VII was nicer to fly from a handling point of view, the Mk XIV was the real performer thanks to its Griffon engine. It was a truly impressive machine, being able to climb almost vertically – it gave many Luftwaffe fighter pilots the shock of their lives when, having thought that they had bounced you from a superior height, they were astonished to find the Mk XIV climbing up to tackle them head-on. It was simply a matter of turning into them, standing the aircraft on its tail and opening the throttle to climb up and engage the enemy. I would love to have had a whole wing of these aircraft.

SPITFIRE FR XIVE NH749

This aircraft was part of a mixed batch of 225 Mk VIIIs and XIVs ordered on 1 December 1942. Built at Aldermaston in early 1945, the fighter was delivered to No 33 MU at nearby Lyneham on 23 February. Stored for three months, the aeroplane was sent to No 215 MU at Dumfries on 30 May for packing and then delivered to No 3 Packed Aircraft Transit Pool four days later. NH749 was duly loaded onboard the Liberty ship SS *Samsturdy*, which sailed for Karachi on 2 July – it reached its destination 26 days later. Received by ACSEA on 9 August, it is doubtful if the aeroplane was ever issued to a frontline RAF unit. However, it appears to have been on strength with the 'Spitfire Flight' of No 151 OTU at Peshawar when the unit amalgamated with the RIAF's No 1 Service Flying Training School (SFTS) and transferred its aircraft

(including nine Mk XIVs) to Ambala. Following India's independence on 15 August 1947, the SFTS was re-designated the Advanced Flying School as part of the newly established IAF.

NH749 fired its guns in anger from late October 1947 when, following the invasion of Jammu and Kashmir by Pakistani troops, the fighter was flown to Srinagar as part of No 1 Ad Hoc Squadron – here, it served alongside Spitfire LF VII MT719, featured earlier in this book. Attacking Mujahideen and Pakistani forces, NH749 and a small number of other Mk XIVs were eventually withdrawn from the action on 10 November due to the difficulties pilots faced operating the Griffon-engined Spitfires from the short and narrow airstrip at Srinigar. NH749, along with all RIAF aircraft, was officially

BELOW NH786, like NH749, was one of a large number of Spitfire F/FR XIVEs (and Spitfire VIIIs, Harvard IIBs and Oxford I/IIs) that were handed over to the RIAF's No 1 AFS by ACSEA's No 151 OTU at Peshawar in March 1946. Photographed here still in its RAF markings, with the addition of large white numerals added by the training unit, this aircraft was written off by Pilot Officer S. M. S. Haque in a belly landing following an in-flight engine failure on 2 August 1946. (via Peter R. Arnold)

RIGHT The most famous Spitfire XIV to see service with South East Asia Command (SEAC) was RN135 of Squadron Leader J. H. 'Ginger' Lacey, CO of No 17 Squadron. Unhappy with the bubble-canopy FR XIVes initially supplied to the unit (upon seeing the first one sent to Madura he exclaimed that it 'wasn't a bloody Spitfire'), Lacey demanded, and received, high-back F XIVes in their place. Seen in Singapore following the Japanese surrender, this aircraft is marked up with Lacey's impressive 28-victory tally beneath the cockpit. This aeroplane remained the CO's mount until he left the squadron in May 1946. On the last day of the previous month he had been at the controls of RN135 when it became the first Spitfire to fly over Japan. (via Peter R. Arnold)

transferred to the IAF on 29/31 December 1947. It remained in frontline service until early 1951, when the surviving Spitfire XIVs (and Mk VIIIs too) were withdrawn from use and issued to NCC units and technical establishments.

NH749 was one of eight Spitfires offered for sale by the Indian government in 1977 (as was MT719), and when it was inspected by Ormond Haydon-Baillie at Patna that same year the engineless airframe was sitting on bricks next to the River Ganges. Acquired, along with the remaining seven Spitfires, shortly after Haydon-Baillie's death, NH749 was shipped to the UK in early 1978 and stored at Wroughton, in Wiltshire. Bought by Spencer Flack shortly thereafter, the aeroplane was moved to Elstree, in Hertfordshire, and then sold to A and K Wickenden. They in turn commissioned Craig Charleston to rebuild the fighter, which made its first post-restoration flight from Cranfield, in Bedfordshire, on 9 April 1983. Although it failed to sell at Christie's Duxford auction later that same month, NH749 was eventually sold to David Price. Shipped to his Santa Monica, California, base, the fighter was loaned for a short while to the co-located Museum of Flight and also took part in the Phoenix Air Races of 1995. The fighter was acquired by the Commemorative Air Force of Camarillo, California, in 2005, and it returned to the air in 2011 following a lengthy renovation and restoration programme that saw its Griffon engine overhauled by Vintage V-12s following an in-flight coolant failure.

NH749 has been marked up in ACSEA camouflage since its restoration more than 30 years ago, this scheme reflecting the colours worn by Spitfire XIVs based in India at war's end. Flight Lieutenant Don Healey was amongst the RAF pilots to fly the Mk XIV in India during the final months of the conflict with Japan, serving with No 17 Squadron at Madura, in southern India:

We had originally been allocated bubble-canopy FR XIVs, but when the first one arrived at Madura in June 1945 my CO, Squadron Leader 'Ginger' Lacey [a 28-victory ace], exclaimed that it 'wasn't a bloody Spitfire'. Despite our protestations concerning the unrivalled visibility out of the canopy, 'Ginger' wouldn't budge, and they were passed on to No 11 Squadron [at nearby Chettinad], whose pilots were more than happy to receive them in place of their war-weary Hurricane IICs. Eventually, we got our complement of high-back F XIVEs, which finally satisfied our boss.

The Mk XIV was a hairy beast to fly, and it took some getting used to. I personally preferred the old Mk V from a flying standpoint. We were fortunate to be based at Madura when we received our first Mk XIVs, as the runway there was more than 3,000 yards long, and fully concreted. It had been an important base for RAF Liberator units bombing Burma and Malaya in 1944/45, and was ideally suited for a squadron coming to grips for the first time with the vicious torque swing of the Griffon

engine. We were told to open the throttle very slowly at the start of our take-off, with full opposite rudder applied to offset the five-bladed prop, which was driven by the Griffon in the opposite direction to the Merlin – this took some getting used to! Even with full aileron, elevator and rudder, this brute of a fighter still took off slightly sideways. However, once you picked up flying speed, and trimmed the rudder and elevator, this torque pull became bearable.

NH749 has worn an ACSEA Temperate Land Scheme since it was restored to airworthiness by Craig Charleston in the early 1980s, these markings reflecting the colours worn by Spitfire XIVs based in India at war's end.

This was the condition NH749 was found in at Patna by Ormond Haydon-Baillie in 1977 – an engineless airframe sitting on bricks next to the River Ganges. The last vestiges of its IAF roundel and RAF serial can just be made out on the fighter's sun-bleached fuselage. (Wensley Haydon-Baillie via Peter R. Arnold)

One aspect you always had to bear in mind with the Mk XIV that no flying surface trimming could allow for was its considerable weight – it tipped the scales at 8,475 lbs when fuelled and armed, which made it more than 2,000 lbs heavier than a Spitfire Mk VIII. Therefore, extra height had to be allowed for when rolling and looping, as it tended to 'wash out' when being flown in this way. 'Ginger' Lacey graphically showed us all just how serious a problem this was when he attempted to do a loop from what he thought was an adequate starting height, and with sufficient speed, over Madura one afternoon. Lacey recounted his brush with death in his autobiography, *Ginger Lacey – Fighter Pilot*, published in 1962:

'Half way up the loop, I realised that I had gone into it much too slowly and I wasn't going to make it. As she approached the top of the loop, on her back, I was frantically trying to roll her out because I knew she was going to stall. And of course, with full aileron on, not only did she stall inverted but she spun inverted. I was only at 2,500 ft. I knew what to do, but it took some doing. I forced her nose down, still upside-down, and let her pick up speed. When she had enough speed, I rolled her out. By that time, I didn't have very much height left. I've never been closer to being killed.'

At the bottom of the loop Lacey cleared the ground by barely four feet, and upon recovering back at the field he looked ten years older than when he took off. He immediately gathered us around and told us in no uncertain terms not to attempt a similar manoeuvre with anything less than a 4,000-ft reading on the altimeter.

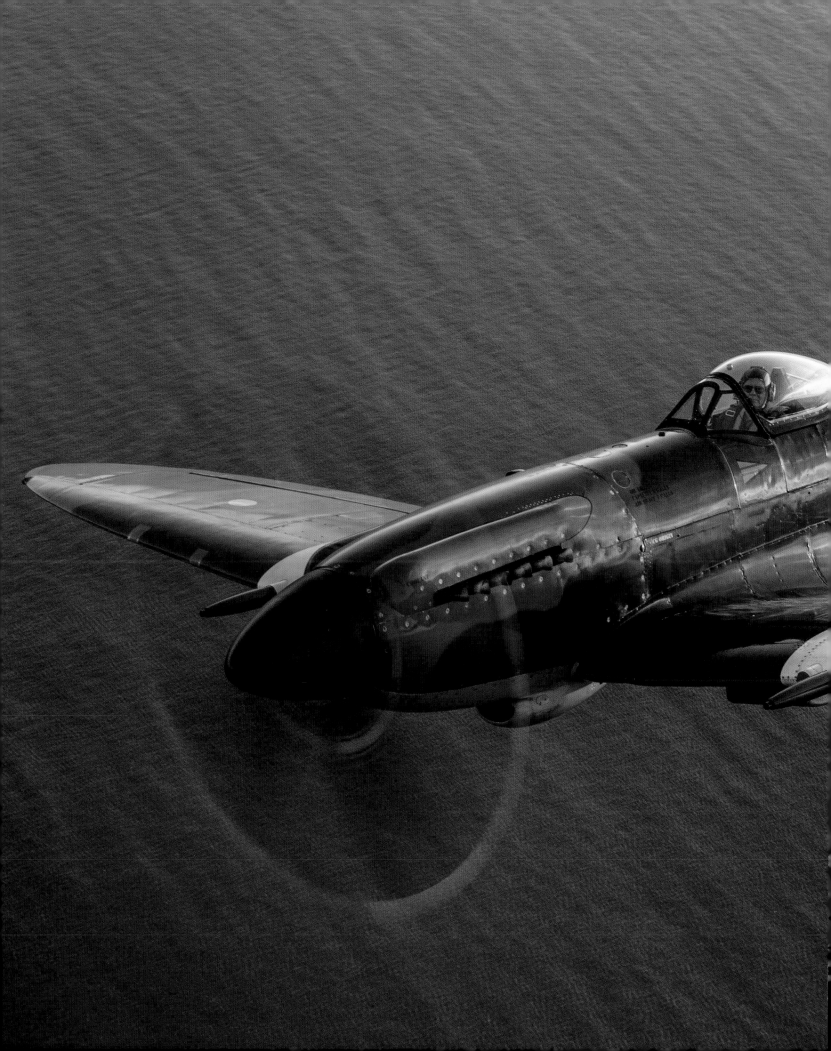

The fighter was acquired from long-term owner David Price by the Southern California Wing of the Commemorative Air Force (CAF) in 2005, and it returned to the air in 2011 following a lengthy renovation and restoration programme that saw the fighter's Griffon engine overhauled by Vintage V-12s following an in-flight coolant failure.

CAF pilot Steve Barber formates with the camera aircraft as the sun sets in the west on a typically beautiful Southern California evening. Barber, a very experienced warbird pilot, was at the controls of NH749 when it suffered its coolant leak. He calmly nursed the aircraft back to its Camarillo home and carried out an uneventful landing. Mike Nixon and his team at Vintage V-12s subsequently determined that the Griffon's entire coolant system had to be refurbished. Whilst the engine was out of the airframe, CAF engineers at Camarillo replaced the wing and undercarriage attachment bolts, repaired the canopy, overhauled the hydraulic, pneumatic and electrical systems and repainted the cockpit and engine compartment in authentic factory colours.

SPITFIRE FR XVIII SM845

Constructed at Eastleigh in the spring of 1945, SM845 was part of an order for 150 Spitfire PR XIs dated 12 February 1944. In the event, a mixed batch of Mks XIV and XVIIIs were built instead, with this Griffon 66-powered machine being delivered to No 39 MU at Colerne, in Wiltshire, on 28 May. The Spitfire remained here in storage until 13 December, when it was flown to the packing unit at No 76 MU at nearby Wroughton and carefully prepared for shipping to India. Loaded onboard the SS *Sampenn* in January 1946, SM845 arrived in Karachi on 11 February and was taken on charge by ACSEA 17 days later.

Transferred to the newly formed IAF on 31 December 1947 as part of a batch of 57 Spitfire XVIIIs 'found' at No 320 MU in Karachi, the fighter – given the serial HS687 – served with No 14 Squadron at Barrackpore, in North Kolkata. Amongst the pilots to fly the aeroplane during the early 1950s was Flying Officer Sharad Thakar, who later saw combat at the controls of a Canberra bomber in the 1965 conflict with Pakistan:

The Spitfire F XVIII was a pilot's aircraft. One could feel the power throb through the fuselage even at the gate of nine inches of boost – across the gate we could get as much as 18 inches. We outperformed the [co-located] Vampires most of the time and had far less [flight] restrictions. Being the last piston engine squadron in the IAF, we tended to be the

butt of all the jokes in the air force. One day in 1957 we could stand it no more, and after the usual taunting flypast by Toofanis (Dassault MD.450 Ouragans) by No 1 Squadron at Kalaikunda, we took up the gauntlet and started up nine Spitfires. After take-off we flew a very tight, very low formation over Kalaikunda just to show them how formation flying was done, followed by the most spectacular beat up of that airfield that lasted about 20 minutes. The Toofanis never came over Barrackpore again.

SM845 was eventually retired to Kalaikunda, near Kharagpur, where it served as a base decoy for many years. The aeroplane was one of eight Spitfires purchased from the Indian Government by the Haydon-Baillie Aircraft and Naval Collection, SM845 being shipped from Bombay to California in March 1978. Sold on to Marshall Moss and Dick Boolootian, it was stored in Lancaster, California, until acquired by David Tallichet in

SM845 is put through its paces by former Red Arrows pilot and CO of the Battle of Britain Memorial Flight Squadron Leader Ian Smith during a late autumn photo-shoot arranged specially for this volume. In the main, the Spitfire FR XVIII was a Mk XIV with strengthened wings and undercarriage and extra fuel tankage. The additional fuel – 66 Imperial gallons in the fuselage and 26.5 Imperial gallons in each wing – made the fighter useful for reconnaissance, for which role it had alternative F24 or F52 camera installations.

1982. Limited restoration work was undertaken on the airframe in Tulsa, Oklahoma, and Casper, Wyoming, between 1984 and 1987, when the fighter was placed in storage at Chino. Bought by David Price shortly thereafter, he in turn sold it to Adrian Reynard who had SM845 shipped back to his home in Woodstock, Oxfordshire – it arrived there on 8 June 1988.

Reynard eventually contracted Historic Flying Ltd (HFL) to complete the fighter's restoration to airworthiness, SM845 being moved to the company's Audley End facility in early 1993. Here, the wings were extensively re-skinned and the fuselage rebuilt. In April 1998 the almost complete Spitfire was sold to Karel Bos of HFL. On 7 July the aeroplane made its first post-restoration flight from Audley End to Duxford, where it was looked after by the Aircraft Restoration Company (ARCo). In January 2009 SM845 was acquired by Biltema AG and flown to Ängelholm, in Sweden. On 21 July 2010 the fighter was damaged in a fatal landing accident at Tynset airfield, in Norway, its pilot, Bertil Gerhardt, being killed when the aircraft came to rest inverted. SM845 was bought by Richard

Lake of Spitfire Ltd in July 2012 and shipped back to HFL/ARCo at Duxford. Its fuselage was then sent to Airframe Assemblies for repair, before being returned to HFL/ARCo for reassembly. The aeroplane made its first flight following its second restoration on 17 December 2013.

Originally flown in No 32 Squadron colours following its first restoration, SM845 was repainted all-silver by HFL/ARCo during its second rebuild to represent an aeroplane serving with No 28 Squadron in the Far East in 1947–48. Flying Officer (later Air Vice Marshal) John Nicholls was assigned to the unit during this period, and he flew the Spitfire FR XVIII in combat in the early stages of the 12-year-long Malayan Emergency that pitched Commonwealth armed forces against the Malayan National Liberation Army (MNLA). Flying from Sembawang, on the island of Singapore, No 28 Squadron, along with similarly equipped No 60 Squadron, provided the bulk of the RAF's offensive strength in the area.

Almost from the start we [and No 60 Squadron] began sending out strikes against the jungle hide-

The first post-war colour scheme promulgated on 16 April 1946 by RAF Fighter Command stated that its aircraft would return to the silver finish of the interwar period – either natural metal or glossy 'silver' (more strictly aluminium) paint work, with black codes and serials. It was many months before this scheme became common in the frontline, and No 28 Squadron, for example, flew camouflaged Spitfire FR XVIIIs alongside 'silver' aircraft well into the late 1940s.

Like the Spitfire XIV before it, the FR XVIII was fitted with the same wing as the Mk VIII, and, as previously noted, they were strengthened in order to cope with the additional 26.5 Imperial gallon tankage in each wing. This extra weight had little effect on the fighter's performance, however, thanks to the fitment of a Rolls-Royce Griffon 67 engine rated at 2,375 hp – an increase of 325 hp over the Spitfire XIV's Griffon 65.

Griffon-engined Spitfires were fitted with enlarged underwing radiators in order to cope with the increased capacity of the Rolls-Royce powerplant. Their layout was also different, with the oil cooler being situated behind the main radiator under the port wing, and the main radiator being behind the intercooler under the starboard wing. And as this photograph clearly shows, the radiators were made deeper than those fitted to Merlin-engined Spitfires. The carburettor air intake immediately beneath the engine remained the same size as that fitted to the Spitfire VIII, however.

The Griffon engine is longer than the Merlin, thus reducing the pilot's visibility over the nose particularly when taxiing on the ground. In an attempt to rectify this problem, Supermarine 'blistered' the top cowling panel to fit over the cylinder blocks and have it lie snugly in the vee between them.

outs used by the terrorists. In the beginning it was a rather hit and miss affair, with one far more likely to miss than to hit. The maps we carried were almost devoid of detail except along the coast – they would show dominant features such as rivers, but after a distance they would peter out into a dotted line with the helpful caption 'It is assumed that the river follows this line'! The reconnaissance Spitfires of No 81 Squadron would take target photographs for us, but since their maps were the same as our own, they had similar problems of navigation. In the jungle one tree-covered hill can look depressingly like a thousand others.

I vividly remember the first time I dropped a bomb in anger. On 2 July 1948 I went off with my squadron commander, Squadron Leader Bob Yule, to a target just across the causeway from Singapore, in South Johore. We took off at first light so that we could get in our dive attacks before the usual mid-morning layer of cumulous cloud developed. When we reached the target area we cruised round for more than half an hour looking for something resembling our briefed objective, before eventually we did attack. Diving from 12,000 ft, we dropped our 500 pounders, two from each aircraft, then we carried out a series of strafing runs with cannon and machine guns. There was no one firing back – it was really like being on the range, except the target was far less distinct.

During the months that followed we flew several similar strikes. Most of the targets were in deep jungle, and sometimes half a dozen of us would circle for up to an hour looking for the huts or whatever it was we were supposed to hit. Then the first pilot who reckoned he had found it would bomb, and the rest of us would follow and aim at his bursts – after that we would strafe the area until we had used up our ammunition. At that time our intelligence on the whereabouts of the enemy was poor. Precision attacks, by definition, require the target to be visible or to be marked in some way.

The ineffectiveness of the Spitfire in these operations illustrates the sort of problem we had, using an interceptor designed 13 years earlier to bomb such difficult targets. Later Lincoln four-engined heavy bombers equipped with radar took over the task of attacking the jungle hideouts, but even with their much greater bomb loads I am not convinced that they achieved much.

I left No 28 Squadron in mid-1949, before the Malayan operations were placed on a proper footing. I had had a lot of fun but had not, I think, done all that much to help defeat the terrorists. Operating against the guerrillas in Malaya, we were really asking too much from the Spitfire. But I have no doubt regarding its value as an air fighter. It had that rare quality which comes from a perfect matching of control responsiveness and 'feel', which made the aircraft part of you once you were airborne. You strapped on, rather than got into, a Spitfire – your hand on the stick produced instant control reaction, and it would obey as accurately and almost as quickly as one's right arm obeys the commands from the brain. I have known a few other aircraft with this particular and highly personal characteristic – the Vampire and the Hunter followed by the F-104A Starfighter, which, despite its outstanding performance in terms of speed, retained that same unique quality as a perfect fighter pilot's aeroplane. But for me the Spitfire was the first and so the one best loved.

SPITFIRE FR XVIII TP280

Ordered in August 1944 and built at Southampton in early 1945, TP280 was one of 20 'Production Prototypes' that were used by the manufacturer to introduce new features into the Spitfire XVIII. Which 'feature' was associated with this particular aircraft remains unrecorded. Completed on 20 March and delivered to No 39 MU at Colerne on 19 June for storage, TP280 was eventually allocated to the Far East Air Force (FEAF) in late 1945. In January of the following year it was sent to No 76 MU at Wroughton for packing and then transported to Birkenhead Docks for loading onto the SS *Tarantia*. The fighter arrived in Karachi on 30 March 1946.

Taken on charge by the RAF in early April, TP280 was again placed in storage until it was allocated for shipment back to the UK in July 1947. However, the newly created IAF had a need for late mark Spitfires, and the aeroplane was brought back on charge at Mauripur, in Karachi, in November 1947. One of 47 Spitfires officially transferred from the RAF to the IAF on 29–31 December, TP280 became HS654 in Indian service and served with No 14 Squadron, and possibly Nos 2, 7 and 15 Squadrons as well. Amongst the pilots to fly Spitfire XVIIIs with No 7 'Battleaxes' Squadron was Pilot Officer (later Group Captain) Kapil Bhargava:

I completed my conversion on Spits and Tempests and joined No 7 Squadron at Palam [in New Delhi] on 7 March 1951. The squadron had just three Vampire III jets, with the rest of its aircraft being Spitfire XVIIIs, and one Harvard for instrument flying and duel checks. My initiation flight in a Spitfire XVIII (HS655) after joining the squadron was for familiarisation, both to refresh my acquaintance with the type and to look over the local flying area.

I had been warned that it was normal practice on the station to bounce unsuspecting aircraft, the

BELOW Spitfire FR XVIII TP280 has been marked up in the colours of this aircraft NH850/'Z' since its restoration to airworthiness in the early 1990s. This particular machine was the personal mount of No 60 Squadron CO, Squadron Leader Duncan-Smith, who was at its controls on New Year's Day 1951 when he led Flight Lieutenant Bailey and Flying Officers Walters and Keogh in a strike on a suspected terrorist hideout near Kota Tinggi, in Malaya. This would prove to be the last operation where a Spitfire of the RAF fired its guns – and rocket projectiles – in anger. Duncan-Smith also led the RAF's first jet strike shortly thereafter. (via Andy Thomas)

LEFT TP280 (wearing its IAF code HS654) has its engine run up on the No 14 Squadron ramp at Barrackpore in June 1955. The unit appears to be preparing for a squadron-strength flight, possibly in response to a taunting flypast of the airfield by Vampire FB 52s of No 1 Squadron, based at nearby Kalaikunda. Parked at the far end of the flightline are a B-24J and a C-47, numerous examples of which served with the IAF well into the late 1950s. (Polly Singh via Peter R. Arnold)

Squadron Leader Wilf Duncan-Smith's Spitfire was adorned with yellow and black nose stripes, a blue/red spinner – unique to the CO's aircraft – and his rank pennant, as well as No 60 Squadron's markhor's head badge on its fin and unit crest below the cockpit.

pilot of which was fined a bottle of beer for consumption in the afternoon. Fourteen pilots on the squadron from the previous course had assured me, however, that I would not be bounced by them for my first few sorties. This assurance was not passed on to our rival neighbours, No 8 'Eighth Pursoots' Squadron, flying Tempests. While I was busy looking at the terrain and generally enjoying the flight, I noticed a Tempest turning in towards my tail. I did not have a clue about what to do but did not want to lose a bottle of beer in my very first fighter sortie in the unit. I decided that if I kept him in sight at all times, he would never get on to my tail. We must have manoeuvred for about ten minutes. He was the cat and I was the mouse. The Spit was easy to handle and the Tempest pilot never got anywhere near to claiming the beer. We landed at about the same time. As he was taxiing past my aircraft, the pilot stuck two fingers up at me. I could not decipher his triumphalist gesture, as he had nothing to crow about. I came to the firm conclusion that while a Tempest could beat the Spitfire in maximum speed, it was not easy, perhaps even unlikely, to beat it in a dogfight.

Following its removal from frontline service, TP280 spent a brief period of time with the Advanced Flying School at Ambala, near Chandigarh. It was eventually retired to Kalaikunda with three other Spitfire XVIIIs, all of which served as decoys. They were eventually acquired by the Haydon-Baillie Aircraft and Naval Collection from the Indian Government in 1977 and shipped from Bombay to California the following year. TP280 (and TP276) had been pre-sold to Rudy Frasca of Champaign, Illinois, and considerable work was carried out on the airframe at Frasca Field over the next 14 years. The wings, however, were sent to the UK for rebuilding by Steve Atkins of Vintage Airworks in Sussex, the tail section was repaired by Airframe Assemblies at Sandown and the Griffon engine was overhauled by Vintage V-12s.

In order to speed up the restoration Rudy Frasca shipped the fuselage of TP280 to HFL at Audley End during May 1991. After 14 months of work the aeroplane made its first post-restoration flight, from Audley End to Duxford, on 5 July 1992. The aeroplane was shipped back to the USA in late August that same year, and it remained in Frasca's ownership until sold to Volker Schulke in February 2015. TP280 was moved to its new home at Bremgarten the following month, where it was reassembled by Meier Motors GmbH and flown for the first time in Germany on 17 June.

The aircraft has worn the colours of No 60 Squadron since its restoration, being finished in the scheme that adorned Spitfire XVIII NH850 whilst it was assigned to Squadron Leader Wilfred Duncan-Smith from July 1949 – indeed, the fighter was signed by a number of No 60 Squadron pilots, including Duncan-Smith, shortly after it had been returned to airworthiness. The peacetime establishment for the RAF in the Far East included several fighter units, including No 60 Squadron based at Tengah, in Singapore. In early December 1946, nightfighter ace Squadron Leader Michael Constable-Maxwell assumed command as the squadron re-equipped with Spitfire FR XVIIIs. The CO collected the first Spitfire after assembly at Seletar-based No 390 MU on 15 January 1947, and No 60 Squadron gradually built up to strength

TOP From July 1948 the Spitfire FR XVIIIs of No 60 Squadron were engaged in attacks on communist terrorists in Malaya during Operation *Firedog* – some 1,800 Spitfire attack sorties were flown during the offensive. The aircraft's final strike was led by the CO, Squadron Leader Wilf Duncan-Smith (right), a wartime ace with 19 victories to his credit. The other pilot in this photograph is Flight Lieutenant Jimmy James, who had flown Hurricanes and Spitfires over Burma in 1942–44 with some success. (via Andy Thomas)

OPPOSITE The 'bubble' canopy fitted to the FR XVIII was a teardrop shape, and provided the pilot with a much improved view aft. The adoption of the canopy necessitated the lowering of the top line of the aft fuselage, and meant extensive structural alterations to the frames and skin. At first the canopy had to be moved fore-and-aft by hand like the original Plexiglas hood, but later a chain-and-cable winding gear was introduced – this was fitted as standard to the FR XVIII.

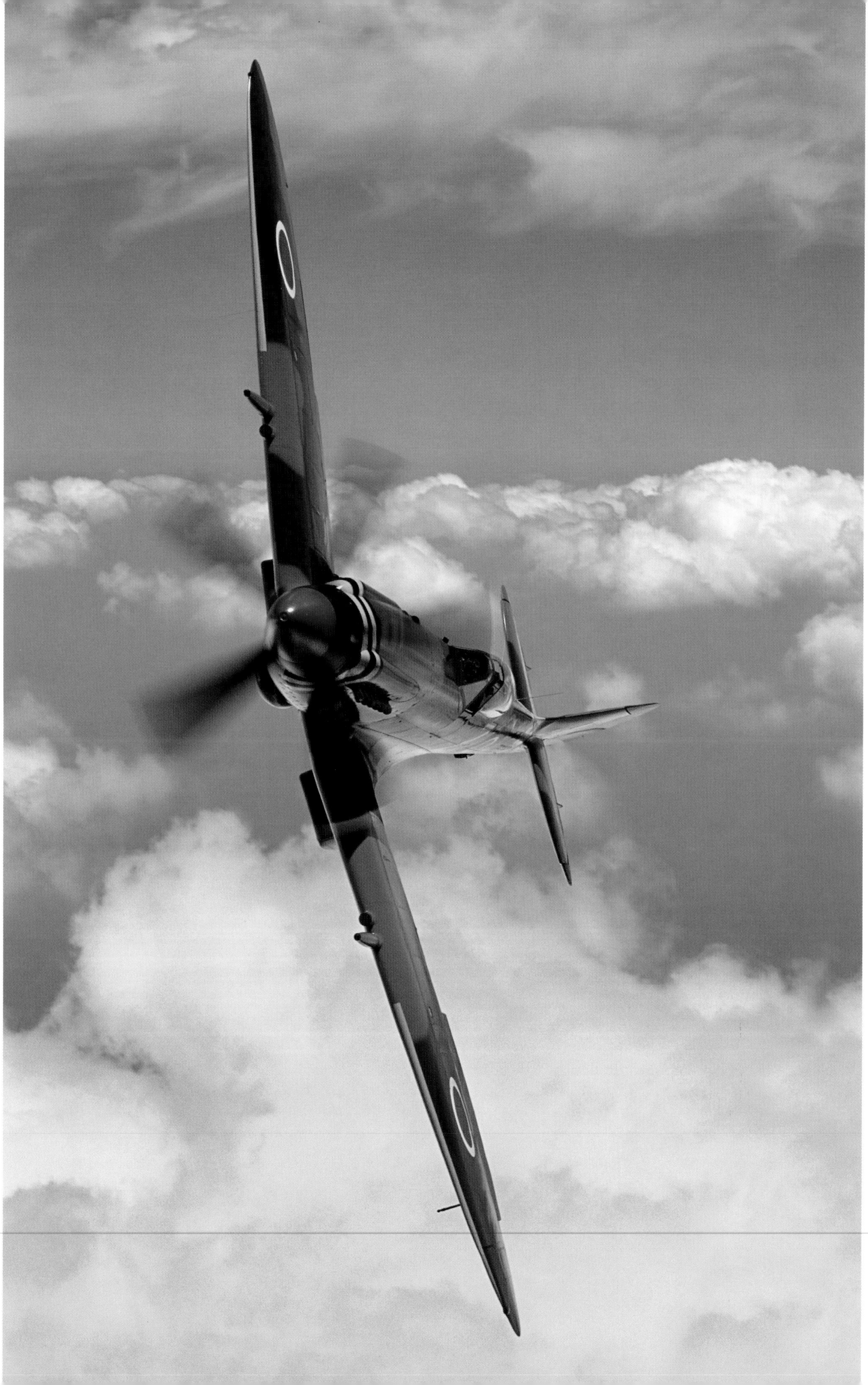

and began flying exercises and bomber affiliation sorties. Constable-Maxwell commented:

Once we got our aircraft into service, life improved for us all. We loved our Spitfires, and the flying was marvellous. We had an establishment of eight aircraft, and No 28 Squadron had the same. When we were asked to give demonstrations, we usually flew as one squadron of 12 aircraft, with Broome, No 28 Squadron's CO, leading the formation while I flew round on my own. I found the best way to get a reaction from spectators was to come over the airfield as fast and low as possible, and just before I reached them, to throttle right back. This resulted in noisy explosions from the open exhausts, and as we were usually inverted at the time, people assumed things had gone wrong!

A peacetime routine was followed, and the following July No 60 Squadron sent six aircraft to Kuala Lumpur to an Army cooperation exercise. Constable-Maxwell left at the end of the year, and in April 1948 permission was given to paint individual peacetime markings on the Spitfires – No 60 Squadron displayed its first personalised aircraft at the Empire Air Day on the 22nd when it showed off its yellow and black stripes around the engine cowling.

Elsewhere, in Malaya, the local colonial administration had, since its reintroduction in 1946, been seriously threatened by the activities of the Malayan Communist Party, who controlled a fairly large and well-equipped force in the jungles of the Malay Peninsula. With acts of terrorism becoming commonplace, on 22 June 1948 a State of Emergency was declared, thus beginning the 12-year-long campaign to suppress it. On 2 July No 60 Squadron detached three aircraft to Kuala Lumpur as part of an RAF Task Force sent to provide air support for the Army. The detachment quickly settled in, and the squadron's Spitfires flew

their first strike on the 6th when they attacked a clearing near Ayer Karah, north of Ipoh. Operation *Firedog* had begun. The unit suffered several losses due to accidents in the subsequent months during periods of varying operational intensity.

One of the largest and most successful air strikes in the early stages of *Firedog* came on 28 February 1949 when eight Spitfires and four Beaufighters hit a group of terrorists in southern Pahang, killing nine.

As previously noted, in early July No 60 Squadron's CO, Squadron Leader Charles Broughton (who received a DFC for his exploits during *Firedog*) was replaced by 19-victory World War 2 ace, Squadron Leader Wilfred Duncan-Smith. Due to the tempo of operations, and following the departure of No 28 Squadron to Hong Kong for policing work the previous year, No 60 Squadron had been increased in size to 16 Spitfires, divided into two flights, by the time Duncan-Smith took over. On 13 October it sent 13 aircraft to Butterworth so that they could fly strikes in northern Malaya, until returning to Kuala Lumpur in early December.

Throughout the year there had been a steady increase in terrorist activity, and this continued into 1950. The squadron increased further in size with the addition of 'C' Flight, comprising three Spitfire PR XIXs for reconnaissance, and these remained until November. However, the ageing Spitfires were increasingly suffering problems with serviceability, and towards the end of the year preparations were being made for No 60 Squadron to become the FEAF's first jet fighter squadron, equipped with Vampires. Then, on New Year's Day 1951, Squadron Leader Duncan-Smith (in NH850/'Z') led Flight Lieutenant Bailey and Flying Officers Walters and Keogh in a strike on a target near Kota Tinggi. This would prove to be the last operation where a Spitfire of the RAF fired its guns in anger. The final remaining FR XVIIIs were replaced by Vampire FB 5s a few days later.

The appreciably increased thrust of the Griffon engine meant that the Spitfire needed a propeller with greater diameter to effectively absorb all that power. As a larger-diameter four-bladed propeller was out of the question for the aeroplane owing to its already small ground clearance, Rotol produced a five-bladed constant speed propeller instead.

CHAPTER EIGHT
SEAFIRES

SEAFIRE LF IIIC PP972

Just one of 250 Type 358 Seafire LF IIICs ordered from Westland Aircraft in July 1943, PP972 left the company's Yeovil factory in Somerset in the summer of 1944. The fighter was transferred to 809 Naval Air Squadron (NAS) in September of that year, and it subsequently embarked with the unit on board HMS *Stalker*, before cross-decking to HMS *Attacker*. PP972 and 809 NAS re-joined HMS *Stalker* in March 1945. The latter vessel, with PP972 on board, left Gibraltar on 7 March 1945 for HMS *China Bay* in Trincomalee, Ceylon, with the 21st Aircraft Carrier Squadron. Once in-theatre, *Stalker* became part of the Royal Navy's East Indies Fleet, which consisted of six escort carriers. Their mission was to provide air support for Operation *Tiderace* – the liberation of Singapore.

During its time in Ceylon, flying from both *Stalker* and *China Bay*, PP972 was involved in numerous operations as part of *Tiderace* as follows – *Dracula* (providing air cover to support landings in Rangoon in May), *Bishop* (a series of attacks on Japanese coastal bases also in May), *Balsam* (offensive sweeps of Japanese air bases in June), *Collie* (providing air cover over the Malayan coast in July), *Zipper* (providing air cover for landings in southern Malaya in August) and *Jurist* (providing air cover during landings at Port Swettenham on 9 September). PP972 also provided air cover for the fleet when it entered Singapore harbour on 10 September following the surrender of Japanese forces. Throughout this period the fighter wore the codes 'D-6M'.

The ultimate development of the Merlin-engined navalised Spitfire, the Seafire III had played an important role with the Fleet Air Arm during the final months of the war. Indeed, almost a third of the Royal Navy's embarked fighter force on its

'I was pleasantly surprised to find that the aircraft's handling has not been adversely affected by the weight of the Seafire III's wing fold mechanism', noted Richard Grace shortly after he had completed PP972's first test flight on 15 June 2015. 'In fact, its ailerons are particularly light. Landing in the aircraft is also entirely normal, although its Fleet Air Arm-inspired camouflage scheme is a ready reminder of the fact that I am strapped into a Seafire.'

As with the Fleet Air Arm before it, the French *Aéronavale* found the Seafire III a handful when operating the fighter at sea. Like surviving Seafire LF IIIC PP972, this particular aircraft was assigned to *Flottille* 1 and embarked in the carrier *Arromanches* during the late summer of 1948 as the unit worked up prior to deploying with the vessel to Saigon later that same year. The pilot of 'I.F_18' nosed his fighter over at speed upon snagging an arrestor cable, with the Seafire's Merlin 55 being wrenched from its mountings when the aeroplane nosed over. (via Andy Thomas)

A forlorn looking PP972 sits alongside an equally derelict Bloch MB.175T torpedo-bomber in a wired-off compound at Base *Aéronavale* 83 Gavres, near Lorient, in February 1966. The Seafire was moved to the aerodrome at Vannes-Meucon four years later, but the rare Bloch was scrapped. (Jean Frelaut via Peter R. Arnold)

carriers in the Pacific and Indian Ocean from late 1944 consisted of Seafire IIIs. Amongst the pilots to fly the aircraft in combat just prior to war's end was Lieutenant Gerry Murphy of 887 NAS, who claimed two victories in the Seafire's final aerial action of World War 2:

When I first flew the Seafire it was pure exhilaration. Having flown the standard training aircraft, which didn't have anything approaching the speed and response, it was great in a climb and when turning, and you felt really in control. It was extremely responsive. I also flew the Hellcat, which was a very robust aircraft, but it was like flying a steamroller compared to the Seafire. It was big and heavy, but a great warhorse, and it could take an awful lot of

punishment. Compared to the Hellcat, the Seafire was rather delicate. The Hellcat didn't have the response of the Seafire. It was the difference between a racehorse and a carthorse. The Seafire III was about 16 knots faster than the Hellcat and Corsair at low and medium altitudes.

And it was not just Fleet Air Arm pilots who were impressed by the Seafire III. Legendary US Navy test pilot 'Corky' Meyer, who had attended the Joint USAAF/US Navy Fighter Conference of March 1943 at Eglin Army Airfield, in Florida, had the chance to fly an early example at this event:

Without argument, the Spitfire/Seafire configuration was probably the most beautiful fighter ever to emerge from a drawing board. Its elliptical wing and long, slim fuselage were visually most delightful, and its flight

Newly restored PP972 is put through its paces by Richard Grace of Air Leasing Ltd, who, along with experienced engineers Steve Kingman and Dave Puleston, spent three years completing the lengthy rebuild of the Seafire LF IIIC. 'I am glad to report that the aircraft handles beautifully, with very light controls and lots of power', Richard Grace explained. 'It leaps off the ground a lot faster than a Spitfire IX, and this is almost certainly because PP972 is significantly lighter. The Seafire III also benefits from having a four-bladed propeller coupled to the "short" Merlin engine.'

PP972 has been camouflaged in the colours and markings it wore when assigned to 809 NAS in 1945, flying from the escort carrier HMS *Stalker*. This vessel was part of the 21st Aircraft Carrier Squadron, which served with the Royal Navy's East Indies Fleet alongside five other escort carriers during the spring of 1945.

characteristics equalled its aerodynamic beauty.

The Seafire had such delightful upright flying qualities that knowing it had an inverted fuel and oil system, I decided to try inverted 'figure-8s'. They were as easy as pie, even when hanging by the complicated, but comfortable, British pilot restraint harness. I was surprised to hear myself laughing as if I were crazy. I have never enjoyed a flight in a fighter as much before or since, or felt so comfortable in an aircraft at any flight attitude. It was clear to see how so few exhausted, hastily trained, Battle of Britain pilots were able to fight off Hitler's hordes for so long, and so successfully, with it.

The Lend-Lease Royal Navy Wildcats, Hellcats and Corsair fighters were only workhorses. The Seafire III was a dashing stallion!

PP972 returned to the UK onboard *Stalker*, flying off to RNAS Nutts Corner, in Northern Ireland, once the carrier returned to home waters in October 1945. 809 NAS disbanded in January 1946, and following a brief period in storage PP972 was transferred to 767 NAS in May. The unit was initially based at RNAS East Haven, in Tayside, although it soon moved to RNAS Lossiemouth, on the Moray Firth, and then its satellite airfield at Milltown, where the fighter received the Milltown code of '120/MV'.

Precise details of the fighter's remaining time with the Fleet Air Arm are presently unknown. PP972 eventually became one of 65 Seafire LF IIICs delivered to the French *Aéronavale* between January and the summer of 1948, the aeroplanes having been retrieved from storage at RNAS Anthorn, in Cumberland, and serviced and overhauled at Lee-on-Solent, in Hampshire. These war-weary veterans were bought for just £80 each, and 30 of the aeroplanes were supplied in airworthy condition. Although the remaining 35 had been struck off charge by the Royal Navy as fit for spares use only, the *Aéronavale* decided to ferry them by air to Toussus-Le-Noble, in northern central France – remarkably, an operation that was performed without mishap.

PP972 was assigned to *Flottille* 1 (and given the code '1.F.9'), which used it during deck landing practice on board the carrier *Arromanches* (formerly HMS *Colossus*). With the creation of *Flottille* 12 on 1 August 1948, the *Arromanches* had its full complement of Seafires (*Groupement de Chasse Embarquée*) and it left Toulon for Saigon on 30 October 1948. On board were 24 Seafires of 1.F and 12 Dauntlesses of 4.F, as well as six NC.701 Martinet twin-engined transport aircraft that were carried as deck cargo, effectively preventing flying during the long voyage to the Far East. The carrier eventually anchored in the Saigon River on 29 November. Almost all of the aircraft were then disembarked at Bien Hoa, from where the Seafires took part in a variety of reconnaissance flights, but on 10 December they returned to the carrier and headed north for operations in the Gulf of Tonkin.

By mid January 1949 the condition of the Seafires was such that their continued presence could not be justified on operational grounds, and with spare parts almost impossible to find (none had been embarked with the aircraft in France), the *Arromanches* steamed home at the end of the month, leaving the Vietnam conflict to the superior talents of the Hellcat, Helldiver and Corsair. The carrier was reassigned to the Mediterranean, but the Seafires of 1.F and 12.F were judged to be unsuited to deck operations in peacetime and therefore relegated to the shore base at Hyères. With a NATO exercise scheduled for the end of 1949 the LF IIIs were replaced with Griffon-engined Seafire F XVs and the earlier aircraft withdrawn from use.

PP972 appears to have been used for technical training and eventually, after a period of storage at Hyères, was noted in a 'wired off compound' at Base *Aéronavale* 83 Gâvres, near Lorient, parked alongside a derelict Bloch MB.175T. It was first seen by future owner Jean Frelaut during 1965, and in 1970 he managed to buy it at scrap value – the Bloch was scrapped that same day – and his team of enthusiasts moved it to the aerodrome at Vannes-Meucon. The initial survey revealed the airframe to be extremely corroded due to prolonged exposure in maritime climates – a factor which later caused the Fleet Air Arm Museum to reject it as a restoration project. The engine and many

This underside view of PP972 reveals the faired 'A-frame' style arrestor hook attached at the mid-point of the rear fuselage, as well as the wing joints for the mainplane folds on the outer edge of the undercarriage bays. The wings were made to fold upwards, with their tips being drooped. When folded, each wing was locked in place with a single removable jury strut.

components were missing, and it was at this stage that Frelaut decided to strip the remaining paint very carefully in order to reveal the underlying squadron markings, which showed that it had also served with 12.F as '12.F.16' and, possibly, '12.F.2' during its career with the *Aéronavale*.

Close examination of the airframe also revealed parts taken from at least three other Seafires, NN136, NN467 and RX166. The top engine cowling was missing but a Mk IX cowling that could be shortened, a four-blade propeller assembly and a canopy Perspex were gifted to John Frelaut by Neville Franklin and Peter Arnold and were collected by Frelaut's brother from Redbourn on 17 June 1972.

After its arrival at Vannes-Meucon and a further move to Plescop on 17 September 1977, Jean Frelaut and his companions did a remarkable job of restoring the aircraft to static display condition in the markings of *Flottille* 1. In so doing they incorporated components recovered from the wreck of Spitfire I P9374, which had crashed on the beach at Calais on 24 May 1940 and been recovered in September 1980. The parts had been obtained by the *Musée de l'Air* at Le Bourget, which, in turn, passed them on to Frelaut. PP972 was exhibited at the Resistance Museum at St Marcel, near Malestroit, from 1982 until July 1984, when it returned to Vannes-Meucon in July 1984. Here, it was re-sprayed in its original Fleet Air Arm camouflage colours, with different schemes being applied on either side of the fuselage – SEAC markings of 809 NAS on the port side and

Milltown-based 767 NAS colours and codes on the starboard side.

PP972 was sold to well-known English collector Doug Arnold in 1988, arriving at Biggin Hill just before Christmas. Here it remained until 6 July 1989, when the fighter was moved by road to Thruxton, in Hampshire, for rebuilding to flying condition by Aerofab Restorations, The aircraft had been transferred to Trent Aero at East Midlands Airport, Castle Donington, by May 1992, with its owner listed as Precious Metals Ltd of St Peter Port, Guernsey. Ownership changed to Wizzard Investments Limited of Jersey on 26 November 1993, both companies being associated with the late Doug Arnold's son, David Arnold. In December 1994 the airframe was recovered back to Biggin Hill from Trent Aero.

In February 1996 PP972 was transported to HFL at Audley End, although it was soon on the move once again, this time to Hawker Restorations/ AJD Engineering at Earls Colne, in Essex. Transported to Hull Aero at Catfield, near Norwich in July 2000, PP972 was relocated to JME Engineering in Suffolk in June 2007, but by August 2008 it had been relocated to the David Arnold's facility at Greenham Common, in Berkshire, and had still not flown. Finally, on 24 May 2012, PP972 was transferred to the workshops of Air Leasing Ltd at Bentwaters, in Suffolk, to commence a final restoration to airworthy condition. Fitted with a Rolls-Royce Merlin 45 engine, the Seafire III completed its first post-restoration flight on 15 June 2015.

SEAFIRE F XVII SX336

Ordered in April 1944 and built by Westland Aircraft at Yeovil, SX336 was officially handed over to the Royal Navy on 30 April 1946. Delivered to the Receipt and Despatch Unit at RNAS Culham, in Oxfordshire, in May, the aeroplane was transferred to the Aircraft Holding Unit at RNAS Abbotsinch, in Glasgow, on 21 August 1946 for storage. Although briefly test flown here, the fighter was destined never to serve with a frontline unit.

The F XVII was the first example of the Seafire family to feature a cut down aft fuselage and 'bubble' canopy (the final 30 Seafire F XVs had also

boasted this modification) and, more importantly, a long-stroke undercarriage. Legendary test pilot Captain Eric Brown detailed the improvements debuted with the F XVII in his volume *Seafire – From the Cockpit*:

All previous Seafires had been fitted with undercarriages that, apart from minor beefing up, were essentially similar to that of the Spitfire VC, which was, of course, almost 1,700 lbs lighter than the Seafire XV. The new undercarriage was markedly stronger and, in consequence, less prone to breaking under the strain of Seafire weights, but more importantly, the oleo stroke had been lengthened. This not only provided greater propeller clearance on the deck, and thus markedly reduced the Seafire's propensity to 'peck' (the blade tips hitting the deck during arresting), it also offered a lower

Seafire F XVII SX165 of 1831 NAS has shed at least two of its propellers after hitting the barrier, having already lost a chunk of its tail section – to which the arrestor hook was mounted – during a lively landing onboard HMS *Illustrious* on 22 September 1949. Its pilot has taken cover in the cockpit as the fighter heads for the barricade, which has been rigged across the flightdeck to the right of the photograph. 1831 NAS was a Royal Naval Volunteer Reserve unit, being one of four issued with Seafires from the summer of 1947. (Lieutenant J. H. Tickle via Andy Thomas)

The naval aviator at the controls of SX351 was successfully extricated from his near tailless Spitfire F XVII after an eventful landing onboard an unidentified carrier in the early 1950s. This aeroplane was originally assigned to 800 NAS in early 1946, and deployed with unit onboard HMS *Triumph* later that same year (via John Dibbs)

Adorned with Yeovilton 'VL' codes on its fin, Seafire F XVII SX246 sits chocked on the flightdeck of an unidentified Royal Navy aircraft carrier with its engine idling, the naval aviator at the controls waiting his turn to launch. Every viewing point on the vessel's island is crammed with sailors watching the action – and when Seafires were involved, an incident was seemingly never too far away. This aircraft survived its fleet service unscathed, however, and it was eventually placed in storage in July 1955. (via Peter R. Arnold)

rebound ratio. This was a boon for deck landing as it absorbed the bounce that could carry Seafires fitted with the earlier undercarriage over the arrestor wires and into the crash barrier.

Another feature of the later production Seafire XVII was an increase in its potential internal fuel capacity. The reduction in the weight aft resulting from the lowered rear decking permitted the installation of a 33 Imperial gallon fuel tank behind the cockpit, adding some 60 miles to the radius of action, and this tank could be replaced by a pair of F24 cameras. A further change in the fuel system of the F XVII was the introduction of fuel lines in the mainplanes which enabled 22.5 Imperial gallon jettisonable slipper-type tanks to be fitted under the outer mainplanes. Known as 'combat tanks', these could be retained for all manoeuvres, and their application was a bonus stemming from the beefed-up main spar necessitated by the new undercarriage. The ability to carry a heavier underwing load – the 'combat tanks' could be replaced by 250-lb bombs or twice as many rocket projectiles as could be toted before – certainly enhanced the tactical flexibility of the Seafire XVII, although it was viewed somewhat as an interim model pending availability of a Seafire fitted with a two-stage Griffon 60-series engine.

Despite these improvements, the Griffon-engined Seafire remained a handful when operated at sea from a carrier, as Commander Geoffrey Higgs of 804 NAS, embarked in HMS *Theseus*, recalled:

My initial impressions of the Seafire were, firstly, how small it was compared with American aircraft I had flown [during World War 2], and secondly, that it was something of an enigma. In the air it became a part of you, like no other aircraft. It was easy and a joy to fly, with seemingly few vices other than distinctly heavy ailerons and a reluctance to turn at near its maximum speed – this would obviously be a handicap in air-to-air combat. On the ground or in the course of carrier operations, however, things were rather different. Its narrow undercarriage made landing in gusty or cross-wind conditions tricky, whilst taxiing over rough ground required care, particularly with the aircraft's nose-heavy tendency to lurch forward.

The forward fuselage and Griffon VI engine of SX336 are carefully extricated from a pile of scrap in the yard of Joseph Brierley & Sons, in Warrington, on 23 July 1973. (Peter R. Arnold)

In short, the Seafire was at home in the air but not on the ground. As a deck-landing aircraft it possessed the most undesirable qualities imaginable. Apart from the ridiculously narrow undercarriage, which took no prisoners if the pilot landed with 'drift on', the aircraft was uncomfortable in the inevitable turbulence short of the carrier's flightdeck round-down, especially when the margin for a successful landing from the approach speed of around 68 knots was plus or minus two knots. Even near the stall, in the high winds encountered over the flightdeck, the Seafire tended to float when about to touch down, owing to the absence drag in the beautifully clean aircraft. If the view over the nose during a carrier approach is taken into consideration, it all added up to a makeshift carrier aeroplane – which of course it was.

Nevertheless, to a young 19-year-old naval aviator like Midshipman Bernard Pike, who had only just received his 'Wings' prior to joining 764 NAS for Piston/Fighter training, the Seafire XVII was a truly magical aircraft:

If the Sea Fury that we progressed to later was a Rolls-Royce, then the Seafire was Mini Cooper. The relatively confined space in its cockpit together with the power available and the easy manoeuvrability it offered made the aircraft feel almost an extension of one's own body. This was surely what young men dreamt of – and, believe me, we dreamt. We were, of course, so fortunate not to be at war, and this, to be absolutely honest, was playtime. I am sure that people would pay fortunes for thrills that were but ten per cent of those that came our way.

SX336 was never flown from a carrier flightdeck or put through its paces by would-be fighter pilots. Instead, it was downgraded to Ground Instructional use and employed as a technical training aid for Naval Airmen Aircraft Mechanics at RNAS Bramcote, in Warwickshire, in the early 1950s. The Seafire was then moved to the Aircraft Holding Unit at RNAS Stretton, in Cheshire, and used for fire-fighting practice. When this airfield was closed on 4 November 1958, SX336 was sold as scrap to British Aluminium of Latchford Locks in nearby Warrington but ended up in the yard of Joseph Brierley & Sons, also in Warrington. Its remains, along with those of F XVII SX300, were discovered and acquired by Peter Arnold in July 1973. He and Neville Franklin (co-founder of the Newark Air Museum) were joint owners of a collection of parts from Seafire F 46's LA546 and LA564, and they agreed an amicable separation of the partnership that saw Arnold take the principal project (LA564) and Franklin the best of the Seafire F XVII components. Further Seafire pieces continued to

emerge from Brierley's yard over the next four years, with the SX336's rear fuselage not being recovered until December 1977.

SX336, along with parts from other Seafires found in various scrap yards, was sold to Craig Charleston on 6 August 1983 and moved to his premises in Potton End, near Berkhampsted. Work commenced on restoring the aeroplane, incorporating the rear fuselage of LA546, with the project being acquired by Peter J. Wood on 26 June 1984. Charleston continued to work on it under contract in Twyford, Buckinghamshire, and steady progress was made until the aircraft was sold to Tim Manna of Kennet Aviation in June 2001. Alan Purdy was contracted to finish the rebuild off in his facility at Nottingham-Tollerton Airport, the fighter arriving here from Manna's Cranfield facility in October 2002. Painted in Fleet Air Arm colours and wearing Yeovilton 'VL' codes on its fin, SX336 (powered by an ex-Royal Canadian Navy Seafire XV Griffon VI engine 'zero-timed' by Retro-Track & Air) made its first post-restoration flight from Kennet Aviation's North Weald home on 3 May 2006.

SX336 is presently the world's only airworthy Seafire F XVII, and this situation is not likely to change any time soon.

Painted in Fleet Air Arm colours and wearing Yeovilton 'VL' codes on its fin, SX336 (powered by an ex-Royal Canadian Navy Seafire XV Griffon VI engine) cruises above the clouds during a flight from Kennet Aviation's North Weald home. The aeroplane is routinely shuttled from Essex down to Yeovilton, where it operates with the Royal Navy Historic Flight. Former Fleet Air Arm pilot John Beattie is SX336's regular display pilot, and he is seen here at the controls.

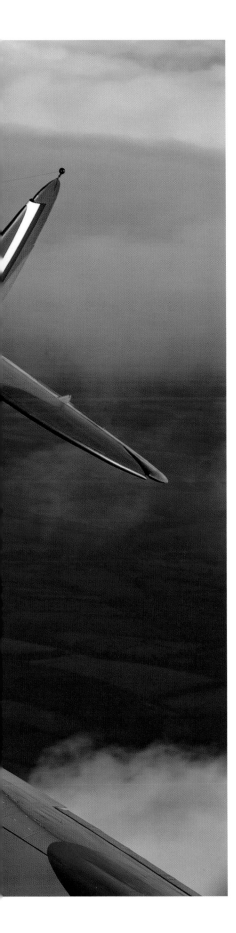

CHAPTER NINE

SPITFIRE SPECTACULAR

Tis final gallery of photographs reveals the sheer number of surviving Spitfires that John Dibbs has photographed 'on the wing' over the past 25 years across the globe. In fact, of the 60-plus examples flying today, he has conducted an air-to-air shoot with more than two-thirds of them. As the images in this book clearly show, the backgrounds against which John poses his subjects are almost as important as the aircraft themselves. Be it high-level cloudscapes, distinctive English countryside or the Channel coast, the 'canvas' upon which the Spitfires have been placed serves to enhance the undeniable beauty of the aeroplane when in its element.

The photographs in this gallery also illustrate the numerous colour schemes worn by the aeroplane both in war and peace, ranging from the early pre-war camouflage adorning Spitfire F IA P9374 to the unique all-silver air racing finish of the Spitfire LF XVIE of No 41 Squadron in the late 1940s. In between are the various colours associated with combat on the Channel Front, the Mediterranean Theatre of Operations, the Far East and high-altitude photo-reconnaissance.

In the final photograph in the gallery a handful of Spitfires are joined by two examples of the RAF's other primary fighter of World War 2, the Hawker Hurricane. Both types fought side-by-side during the early, desperate, years of the conflict, after which the Spitfire replaced the Hurricane in frontline service in most theatres in which the RAF was involved.

Spitfire F IA P9374

Spitfire F IA P9374.

Spitfire F IA P9374

Spitfire F IA P9374.

ABOVE Spitfire FVC AR614 of No 312 'Czech' Squadron at Warmwell.

Spitfire FVC AR614.

Spitfire F VC AR614.

Spitfire F IA AR213.

Spitfire LF VB AB910.

Spitfire F VC (Trop) JG891

Spitfire F VB BM597.

Spitfire LF VB EP120.

Spitfire F VC(Trop) JG891.

Spitfire FVC (Trop) JG891

Spitfire LF IXE Mk 356

Spitfire LF IXE PL344 and Spitfire LF XVIE TD248.

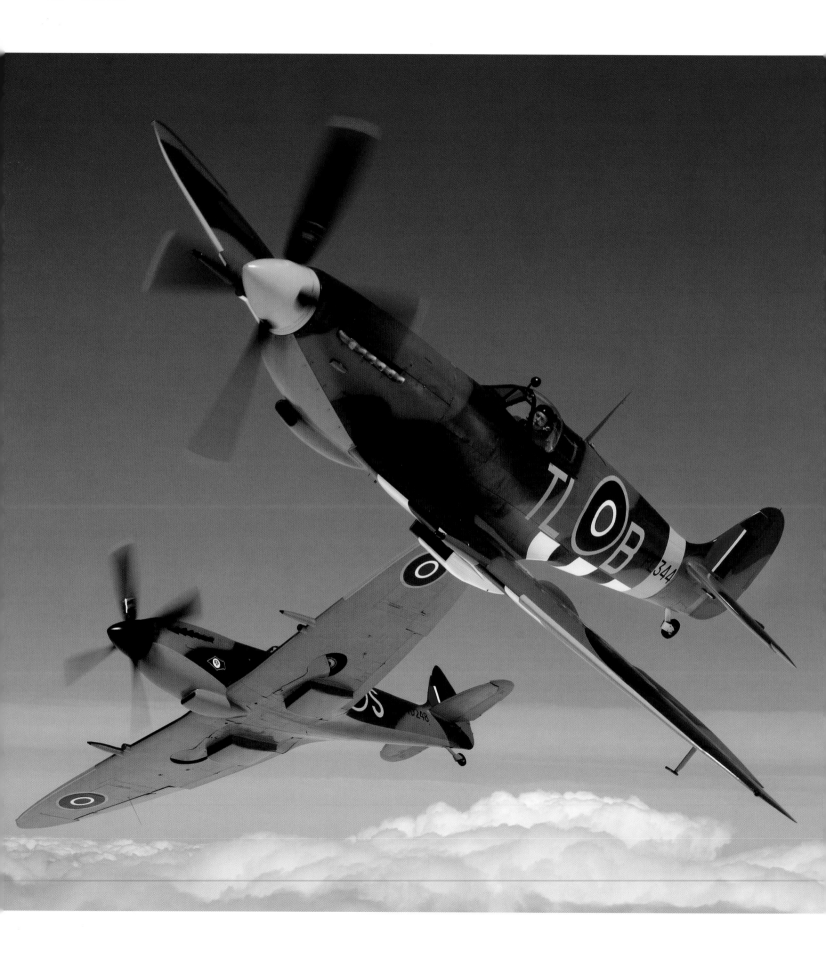

OPPOSITE Spitfire LF IXE PL344
and Spitfire LF XVIE TD248.

ABOVE Spitfire LF XVIE TE184.

RIGHT Spitfire PR XIX PS915.

OPPOSITE Spitfire F XIV RN201 and
Spitfire LF XVIE TD248.

ABOVE Spitfire LF XVIE TE311, Spitfire
F IIA P7350, Spitfire LF IXE MK356,
Spitfire PR XIX PS915 and Spitfire
PR XIX PM631.

RIGHT Spitfire PR XIX PS915.

NEXT PAGES (front vic, right to left)
Spitfire LF XVIE TE311, Spitfire HF
IXE/T 9 SM520, Spitfire F IIA P7350,
Spitfire LF IXE/T 9 and Spitfire LF VB
AB910, (middle) Hurricane IIC PZ865,
(rear vic, right to left) Spitfire FR XVII
SM845, Hurricane IIC LF363 and Spitfire
LF IXE MK356.

CHAPTER TEN

FROM THE ARCHIVE

The following chapter draws together a fascinating collection of archive images, many from private collections, and not often published. They give an intriguing insight into the Spitfire at war.

LEFT No 19 Squadron Spitfire F IAs at Duxford.

ABOVE Squadron Leader Andrew Farquhar, CO of No 602 'City of Glasgow' Squadron, with an He III he helped to shoot down – the first German bomber to crash on mainland Britain.

ABOVE Spitfire F IAs under construction in Southampton.

BELOW Spitfire F IAs of No 611 'West Lancashire' Squadron at Digby.

ABOVE Spitfire F IAs of No 65 Squadron, up from Hornchurch.

LEFT Spitfire F IA force landed on Dunkirk beach.

BELOW Spitfire F IAs of No 611 'West Lancashire' Squadron overfly Digby.

OPPOSITE Spitfire F IA of No 602 'City of Glasgow' at Drem.

OPPOSITE TOP Squadron Leader Andrew Farquhar's Spitfire F IA with victory symbols.

Spitfire F IAs of No 610 'County of Chester' Squadron on patrol from Gravesend.

OPPOSITE TOP Spitfire F VBs of
No 64 Squadron at Hornchurch.

OPPOSITE BOTTOM Spitfire F IA
of No 19 Squadron, Fowlmere.

RIGHT Spitfire F IA
instructional airframe.

BELOW RIGHT Fighter contrails
over Kent on 3 September 1940.

BOTTOM Spitfire F VBs of
No 485 'New Zealand' Squadron
at Kenley. (via Kent Ramsey)

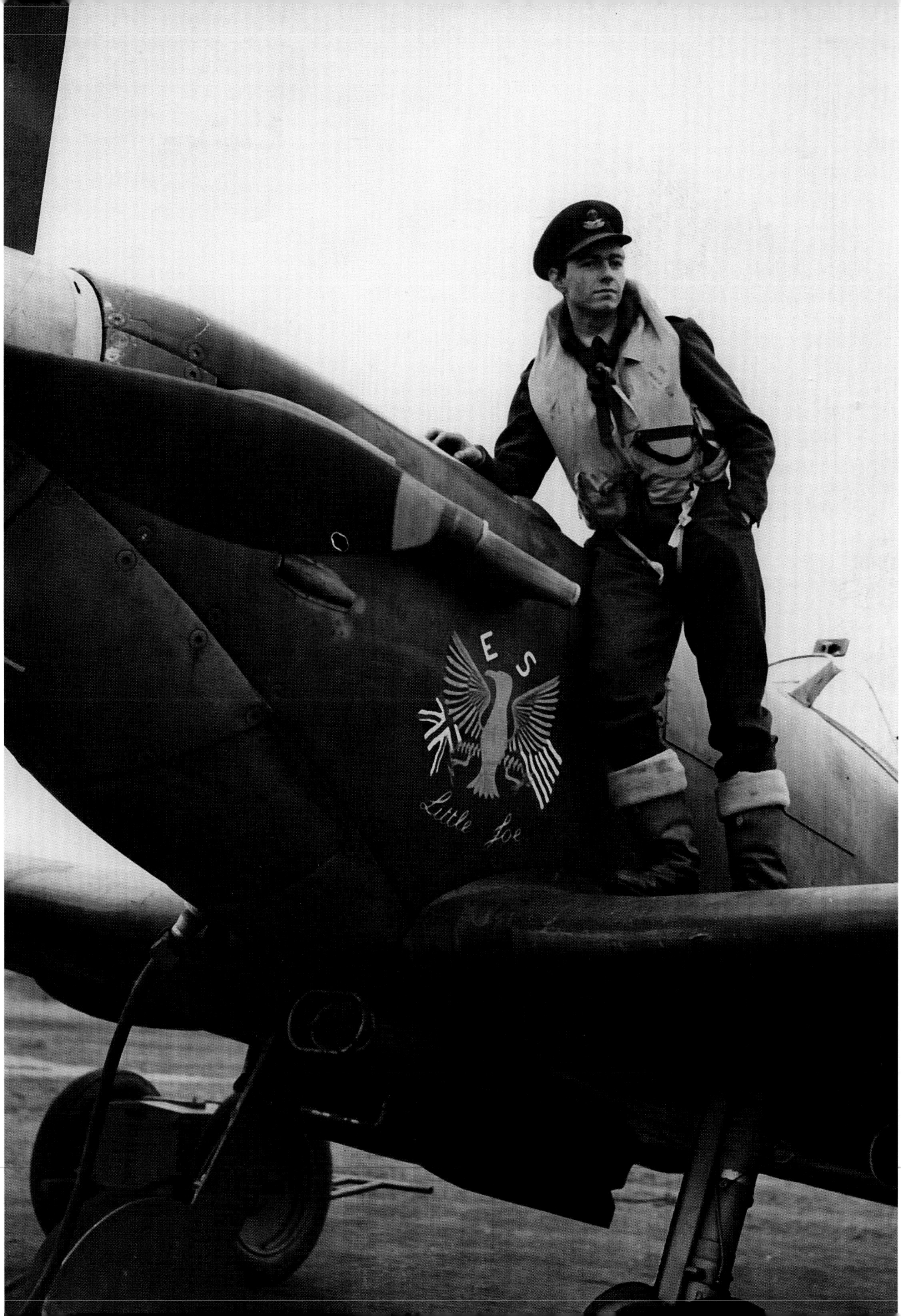
E S
Little Joe

OPPOSITE Pilot Officer J. M. 'Moe'
Kelly of No 71 'Eagle' Squadron,
North Weald. (via Kent Ramsey)

ABOVE Spitfire FVB of the 309th
Fighter Squadron/31st Fighter
Group at High Ercall.

LEFT Spitfire FVBs of No 121
'Eagle' Squadron return to North
Weald. (via John Dibbs)

ABOVE Spitfire F IX of No 611 'West Lancashire' Squadron at Biggin Hill.

LEFT Spitfire F IX of No 332 'Norwegian' Squadron on a beer run from Tangmere.

OPPOSITE Captain Don Willis of the 335th Fighter Squadron/4th Fighter Group at Debden. (via Kent Ramsey)

APPENDICES

SPITFIRE I/IA

Although resembling the handcrafted Spitfire prototype K5054, the jig-built Spitfire I differed significantly from it in a number of key areas, primarily internally. The fighter's distinctive elliptical wing was significantly strengthened so as to raise its never-to-be-exceeded maximum speed from 380 mph to 470 mph. Flap travel was also increased from 57 degrees to 90 degrees, and fuel tankage boosted from 75 to 84 Imperial gallons. Other minor changes were also introduced that ultimately saw the first production Spitfire I weigh in at 5,819 lb fully loaded – 460 lb heavier than K5054.

The first 64 airframes were fitted with Merlin II engines, whilst the remaining Spitfire I/IAs were powered by the 1,030 hp Merlin III. From the 78th airframe onwards, the Rolls-Royce engine would be driving a three-bladed de Havilland or Rotol two-pitch or constant speed propeller, rather than the Watts two-bladed fixed-pitch wooden airscrew. The new propeller improved the take-off run from 420 yards to 225 yards (with the constant-speed propeller), increased the rate of climb, boosted the top speed from 361 mph to 365 mph and made the Spitfire much easier to handle in combat.

The first Spitfire Is reached No 19 Squadron in August 1938, and further modifications were brought in following early months of service flying. Engine start problems were cured with a more powerful starter motor, an engine-driven hydraulic system to raise and lower the undercarriage replaced the hand pump that was originally fitted and a bulged canopy was introduced to provide the extra headroom that was needed to allow taller pilots to fly the aircraft in comfort. Early in World War 2, once it became clear that pilots of modern fighters needed armour protection, the previously unarmoured Spitfire I had a thick slab of laminated glass fitted to the front of its windscreen. A 3 mm thick light alloy cover was also fitted over the upper fuel tank in the fuselage and 75 lbs of steel armour installed behind and beneath the pilot's seat.

In the spring of 1940 the RAF also introduced 100 octane fuel in place of the 87 octane that it had previously used. The Spitfire I's Merlin engine had to be modified to run on this petrol, and the higher octane gave pilots the option to select double the supercharger boost for a maximum of five minutes (raising the top speed by up to 34 mph) without the risk of damaging the

Spitfire F IA.

Merlin III. IFF (Identification Friend or Foe) transponder equipment was also introduced soon after the outbreak of war, thus allowing radar operators on the ground to identify the aircraft they were tracking on their plots. Finally, on the eve of the Battle of Britain, all frontline Spitfires were fitted with 'two-step' rudder pedals, with the upper step six inches higher than the lower step. Just prior to combat, the pilot lifted his feet on to upper steps, thus giving his body a more horizontal posture that in turn raised his blackout threshold by about 1 G, allowing him to sustain tighter turns in action.

In the summer of 1940, non-Castle Bromwich built aircraft that were still equipped with eight Browning 0.303-in machine guns were re-designated Spitfire IAs so as to differentiate them from the recently-introduced cannon-armed Spitfire IB. Production of the Spitfire I ran from April 1938 through to March 1941, by which time 1,567 examples had been built.

DIMENSIONS AND PERFORMANCE DATA FOR SPITFIRE IA

TYPE:	Single-engined monoplane fighter
DIMENSIONS:	Length: 29 ft 11 in (9.12 m)
	Wingspan: 36 ft 10 in (11.23 m)
	Height: 11 ft 5 in (3.48 m)
WEIGHTS:	Empty: 4,810 lb (2,182 kg)
	Loaded Weight: 5,844 lb (2,651 kg)
PERFORMANCE:	Max Speed: 355 mph (571 km/h)
	Range: 575 miles (925 km)
	Powerplant: Rolls-Royce Merlin II/III
	Output: 1,030 hp (768 kW)
ARMAMENT:	Eight 0.303-in machine guns in wings
FIRST FLIGHT DATE:	14 May 1938
PRODUCTION:	1,567

Spitfire F IIA.

SPITFIRE II

Following a series of delays, the massive 'Shadow Factory' established by the Nuffield Organisation in Castle Bromwich at last began to produce Spitfires in June 1940. These aircraft were virtually identical to late-production Spitfire Is built elsewhere in the UK, but they were fitted with the slightly more powerful Merlin XII engine that produced 110 hp more than the Merlin III. Designated the Spitfire IIA, the first examples were delivered to No 611 Squadron in August 1940, followed by Nos 19, 74 and 266 Squadrons. Towards the end of the aircraft's production run at Nuffield, 170 cannon-armed Spitfire IIBs were built at the factory, these aircraft also boasting four 0.303-in machine guns. By the time production of the Spitfire IIA ended in July 1941, 751 examples had been built.

DIMENSIONS AND PERFORMANCE DATA FOR SPITFIRE F IIA

TYPE:	Single-engined monoplane fighter	PERFORMANCE:	Max Speed: 357 mph (574 km/h)
DIMENSIONS:	Length: 29 ft 11 in (9.12 m)		Range: 500 miles (805 km)
	Wingspan: 36 ft 10 in (11.23 m)		Powerplant: Rolls-Royce Merlin XII
	Height: 11 ft 5 in (3.48 m)		Output: 1,175 hp (876 kW)
WEIGHTS:	Empty: 4,900 lb (2,223 kg)	ARMAMENT:	Eight 0.303-in machine guns in
	Loaded Weight: 6,317 lb (2,865 kg)		wings
		FIRST FLIGHT DATE: June 1940	
		PRODUCTION:	921

Spitfire FVC.

SPITFIRE V

The Spitfire V was simply a Mk I airframe fitted with the new Merlin 45, 46, 50 or 50A engine. The Merlin 45 was the less complicated version of the Merlin XX, which powered the Mk III. The supercharger's second stage was removed and a new single-speed single stage supercharger fitted in its place. The Merlin 45 was rated at 1,440 hp on take-off and was easy to mass produce. Other improvements incorporated into the engine included a new carburettor, which allowed for negative-G manoeuvres and no interruption of fuel flow to the engine. Pilots soon found the Merlin 45-powered Spitfire V ran at excessively high oil temperatures. The original engine cooling system of the Spitfire I was not powerful enough, so a larger matrix had to be fitted to the cooler, which in turn required a

larger air intake – the new oil cooler intake was enlarged and made circular in shape. The Spitfire I's fabric ailerons were also replaced with examples made from light alloy.

The first Spitfire Vs built were fitted with the A-type wing that housed eight 0.303-in Browning machine guns. Armour plating was also increased, weighing in at 129 lbs. Top speed for the Spitfire VA was 375 mph at 20,800 ft, and just 94 were built.

The Spitfire VB would ultimately be the most-produced Mk V variant. It featured the B-type wing, which housed two Hispano 20 mm cannon, with 60 rounds per weapon, and four 0.303-in Browning machine guns with 350 rounds per gun. Armour was increased in weight to 152 lbs. Spitfire VA AB320 was converted into a Mk VB and used as the prototype for the first fully tropicalised Mk V. The most visible modification was the addition of the prominent Vokes filter beneath the nose. A tropical radiator and oil cooler were installed, and the aircraft also had provision for an external slipper tank of 90 Imperial gallons. Other internal changes included the addition of tropical survival gear, which consisted of a 1.5 Imperial gallon tank filled with drinking water and a container for flying rations, a signal pistol and cartridges, an emergency tool roll and a heliograph mirror and ground signalling strips. Air tests revealed that the Spitfire VB Trop fitted with a Merlin 45 engine had a top speed of 337.5 mph at 17,400 ft. Rate-of-climb was 2,145 ft per minute, with a ceiling of 34,500 ft.

The Spitfire VC introduced the 'universal' C-type wing that was first tested on the Spitfire III prototype. This variant also featured all of the tropical modifications found on the VB Trop. The 'universal wing' was designed to reduce manufacturing time and allowed for three different armament options. The 'C' wing featured either eight 0.303-in machine guns, two 20 mm cannon and four 0.303-in machine guns or four 20 mm cannon. The Hispano Mk II cannon were now belt fed from box magazines, thus doubling the ammunition per weapon to 120 rounds. Early-build Spitfire VCs were delivered with four 20 mm cannon, but two of these weapons were usually removed once the fighter was in frontline service. Later, production would shift back to the B-type wing of two 20 mm cannon and four 0.303-in machine guns.

The airframe of the Spitfire VC was also re-stressed and strengthened, and it introduced the new laminated windscreen design as seen on the Mk III. Metal ailerons were fitted as standard, along with a stiffened undercarriage with wheels that had been moved two inches forward. Armour was increased to 193 lbs. To increase the Spitfire VC's ferry range a 29 Imperial gallon fuel tank was installed behind the pilot. This, combined with a 90 Imperial gallon slipper tank, meant that the Mk VC could carry up to 204 Imperial gallons of fuel, which gave it a ferry range of approximately 700 miles. When fitted with four 20mm cannon, the Spitfire VC had a top speed of 374 mph at 19,000 ft. The Mk VC served mainly in overseas theatres, including the Middle East, Burma and Australia.

In order to improve the low-level performance of the Spitfire V, a number of Mk VB airframes were modified and fitted with either the Merlin 45M, 50M or 55M powerplant. The 'M' suffix denoted a Merlin engine equipped with a cropped supercharger blower that worked best at lower altitudes – indeed the motor gave its optimum performance at 6,000 ft. The airframe was also modified, with the Spitfire's famous pointed wingtips being removed to reduced the wingspan to 32 ft 6 in. The new square-tipped wings gave the LF (Low Altitude Fighter) V a greater diving speed, better acceleration and faster rate-of-roll when compared to a standard Spitfire V. Many LF Vs were used Mk VB airframes taken from storage and duly modified. Due to the aircrafts' previous service, the LF Vs were soon nicknamed 'the clipped, cropped and clapped Spittys'. At low altitude the LF V had a maximum speed of 338.5 mph at 2,000 ft and 355.5 mph at 5,900 ft.

The Mk V version of the famous Spitfire would be built in greater numbers than any other variant. It would be powered by nine different types of Merlin 45 engine and would see action on every front. The Mk V would also be navalised and transformed into the Seafire IB, IIC and III.

DIMENSIONS AND PERFORMANCE DATA FOR SPITFIRE F VC

TYPE:	Single-engined monoplane fighter
DIMENSIONS:	Length: 29 ft 11 in (9.12 m)
	Wingspan: 36 ft 10 in (11.23 m)
	Height: 11 ft 5 in (3.48 m)
WEIGHTS:	Empty: 5,100 lb (2,313 kg)
	Loaded Weight: 6,785 lb (3,078 kg)
PERFORMANCE:	Max Speed: 374 mph (602 km/h)
	Range: 470 miles (756 km)
	Powerplant: Rolls-Royce Merlin 45/50/55/56
	Output: 1,470 hp (1,096 kW)
ARMAMENT:	Eight 0.303-in machine guns or four 20 mm cannon in wings; provision for one 500-lb (227 kg) or two 250-lb (113 kg) bombs externally
FIRST FLIGHT DATE:	December 1940
PRODUCTION:	6,472

Spitfire HF VIII.

SPITFIRE VII/VIII

Despite having earlier mark numbers the Spitfire VII and VIII actually entered service well after the Mk IX due to the substantial redesign embodied in both variants. Utilising the Merlin 60 and 70 series engines (with their two-stage, two-speed supercharger), six-port exhaust, four-bladed propeller, longer nose and symmetrical underwing radiators, the Mk VII/VIII combined these powerplant improvements with a reworked and strengthened fuselage, revised universal 'C' wing that was fitted with shorter span ailerons and additional fuel tankage. Most aircraft also had a distinctive pointed fin and rudder of a larger area in order to offset the extended protuberance of the engine. Strengthened engine mounts and undercarriage struts were introduced with the Spitfire VII/VIII, as was the retractable tail-wheel unit designed for the stillborn Spitfire III.

The Mk VII was built as a specialist high-altitude interceptor, with extended wing tips and a pressurised cabin, whilst the Mk VIII was built to an identical specification, but lacked both of these features as it was intended to be a conventional fighter-bomber. As with earlier marks of Spitfire, alternative engines were installed in both Mks VII and VIII. In the case of the latter aeroplane, the Merlin 61, 63 or 63A was fitted in the F VIII, the Merlin 66 in the LF VIII and the Merlin 70 in the HF VIII.

The Mk VII started to enter squadron service in September 1942, and the fighter scored its first kill later that same month at 38,000 ft (11,580 m). The Mk VIII made its service debut in 1943, and went on to equip units in the Mediterranean, the Balkans, the Middle and Far East and Burma. Aside from the RAF, the Royal Australian Air Force was the major user of the Mk VIII, receiving 410 examples from October 1943.

DIMENSIONS AND PERFORMANCE DATA FOR SPITFIRE LF VIII

TYPE:	Single-engined monoplane fighter
DIMENSIONS:	Length: 31 ft 3.5 in (9.54 m)
	Wingspan: 36 ft 10 in (11.23 m)
	Height: 12 ft 7.75 in (3.86 m)
WEIGHTS:	Empty: 5,800 lb (2,631 kg)
	Loaded Weight: 7,767 lb (3,523 kg)
PERFORMANCE:	Max Speed: 404 mph (650 km/h)
	Range: 1,180 miles (1,900 km)
	with external tanks
	Powerplant: Rolls-Royce Merlin 66
	Output: 1,720 hp (1,282 kW)
ARMAMENT:	Two 20 mm cannon and four
	0.303-in machine guns in wings;
	provision for 1,000-lb (454 kg)
	bombload externally
FIRST FLIGHT DATE:	May 1942
PRODUCTION:	1,658

Spitfire F IX.

SPITFIRE IX

The Mk IX was built as an interim version whilst development continued on the re-engineered Mks VII and VIII, the frontline Spitfire Vs being progressively outclassed by the Bf 109F/G and, in particular, the Fw 190. RAF Fighter Command desperately needed a new Spitfire to redress the balance, and the quickest way to do this was to marry the new Merlin 61 engine with a lightly modified Spitfire VC airframe. Changes introduced included the strengthening of the fuselage and undercarriage and revision of the radiator system. The geometry of the undercarriage was altered slightly for centre of gravity considerations, and the intercooler fitted to the Merlin 61 necessitated a radiator. The new layout for the radiators put a main coolant radiator and the intercooler radiator under the starboard wing and a main coolant radiator and oil cooler under the port wing. In this way the cooling system was split, and was symmetrical along each side of the engine and airframe.

Although it was the Mk VC that was converted into the Mk IX, the armament of the latter aircraft was fixed at two 20 mm cannon and four 0.303-in machine guns so as to expedite production.

The rapid creation of the Mk IX meant that it was in service well before either the Mk VII or VIII. With a maximum overload take-off weight of 9,500 lbs, the fighter could attain 408 mph in level flight. This mark

had such good performance, and became so popular, that many more than the planned number were eventually built. The type had such a long life that several variants made their bow. Initially, the Mk IX had either a Merlin 61, 63 or 63A engine installed, although the Merlin 66 was subsequently introduced for optimum speed at lower altitudes – this variant was called the LF IX. For optimum speed at higher altitude, the installation of the Merlin 70 created the HF IX. Both the Merlin 66 and 70 had the Bendix Stromberg injection type carburettor instead of the normal gravity-feed carburettor, and also different supercharger gear and propeller reduction gear ratios.

To obviate the need for a tropical air intake conversion set (as seen on the Mk V), a new air intake assembly which included a filter was introduced. A shutter in the forward-facing intake could be operated by the pilot to allow air to pass straight through to the carburettor, or to divert the air through the filter before it entered the carburettor. The duct and filter unit fitted snugly under the engine, and was enclosed by the bottom cowling panel.

The Mk IX was later chosen to be the first in the range to carry 0.5-in Browning machine guns. The 'universal' C-type wing had two 20 mm gun bays, but only the inboard one was used when the mixed armament was carried. This 20 mm weapon was now moved to the outboard bay, and the 0.5-in machine gun installed in the inboard bay. The 0.303-in machine guns were deleted. The change in armament meant a change in nomenclature, and the suffix E was added to the mark number. As the 0.5-in guns were fitted to LF and HF aircraft only, the new list of variants was the F IX, LF IX, LF IXE, HF IX and HF IXE.

A further improvement in connection with the armament was the introduction of the Gyro gunsight to later Mk IXs. This eliminated a good deal of the human element when it came to aiming the guns, although it added quite a lot more 'furniture' to an already very full cockpit.

The versatility of the Mk IX was still not exhausted, however, and in addition to a Mk V-type drop tank or bomb, the aeroplane could carry a 250-lb bomb under each wing at the 20 mm cannon position.

DIMENSIONS AND PERFORMANCE DATA FOR SPITFIRE F IX

TYPE:	Single-engined monoplane fighter
DIMENSIONS:	Length: 31 ft 1 in (9.47 m)
	Wingspan: 36 ft 10 in (11.23 m)
	Height: 12 ft 7.75 in (3.86 m)
WEIGHTS:	Empty: 5,800–6,200 lb (2,631–2,812 kg)
	Max T/O: 9,500 lb (4,309 kg)
PERFORMANCE:	Max Speed: 408 mph (657 km/h)
	Range: 980 miles (1,577 km) with external tanks
	Powerplant: Rolls-Royce Merlin 61
	Output: 1,565 hp (1,167 kW)
ARMAMENT:	Two 20 mm cannon and four 0.303-in machine guns in wings; provision for 1,000 lb (454 kg) bombload externally
FIRST FLIGHT DATE:	early 1942
PRODUCTION:	5,665

Spitfire PR XI.

SPITFIRE PR XI

Early photo-reconnaissance Spitfires were adaptations of the Mks I and V fighter airframes, originally referred to as Spitfires Types A to G. However, from the summer of 1941 until the advent of the PR XI in the autumn of 1942, the main workhorse of the PR units was the PR IV. This was basically an unarmed, unarmoured Mk V fighter with the current Merlin 45 or 46 powerplant. Most were conversions from fighters (there was only ever a small run of true production Mk IVs) and, broadly speaking, PR status resulted from the fitting of cameras and special

wings with leading edge fuel tanks (each with a capacity of 66.5 Imperial gallons) forward of the mainspar, which gave the PR IV a total capacity of 218 Imperial gallons (including fuselage tanks). This, therefore, gave the aeroplane a greatly increased radius of operations.

By the summer of 1942 the Spitfire IX was beginning to re-equip Fighter Command squadrons, the new aeroplane being welcomed for its vastly enhanced rate of climb and power at altitude. This was conferred by the Merlin 60 series engine, the spectacular improvement in performance being produced by its two-speed, two-stage supercharger. When fitted with the Merlin 70 series, the Mk IX benefited from a Rolls-Royce Bendix-Stromberg carburettor that injected fuel into the 'eye' of the supercharger.

The PR XI that evolved during the course of 1942 can be described as a Mk IX without armament and some armour – indeed the first 15 urgently produced by No 1 PRU in the autumn of that year were conversions from standard Spitfire IXs. The new aeroplane had the PR IV's wing leading edge tanks and an increased oil capacity – the enlarged oil tank beneath the engine gave the PR XI its distinctive 'chin' profile. The aeroplane also had a drag-reducing retractable tail-wheel (similar to that fitted to the Mks VII and VIII) and a one-piece wrap-around windscreen in place of the bullet-proof example employed by the Mk IX.

A variety of camera combinations were possible in the PR XI in a 'U' (universal) installation situated between the rear fuselage frames 13, 14 and 15. Two vertical cameras ('fanned' F8 20-inch, which was later replaced by the F52 20- or 36-inch camera, or 'fanned' F24 14-inch) could be installed, with an oblique camera (again, F24 14-inch) above. The vertical cameras were principally used for surveillance, mapping and bomb damage assessment from medium to high altitude. They were normally matched and vertically 'fanned' to port and starboard so that two overlapping photographs could be taken simultaneously. The oblique camera was intended for medium to low-level tactical work. The camera ports were covered by quarter-inch plate glass. Late-build PR XIs also had an F24 five-inch camera installed in a blister attached to the underside of each wing.

DIMENSIONS AND PERFORMANCE DATA FOR SPITFIRE PR XI

TYPE:	Single-engined monoplane photo-reconnaissance aircraft
DIMENSIONS:	Length: 31 ft 1 in (9.47 m)
	Wingspan: 36 ft 10 in (11.23 m)
	Height: 12 ft 7.75 in (3.86 m)
WEIGHTS:	Empty: 5,630 lb (2,553 kg)
	Max T/O: 8,700 lb (3,946 kg)
PERFORMANCE:	Max Speed: 422 mph (679 km/h)
	Range: 1,360 miles (2,188 km)
	Powerplant: Rolls-Royce Merlin 70
	Output: 1,710 hp (1,275 kW)
ARMAMENT:	None
FIRST FLIGHT DATE:	November 1942
PRODUCTION:	471

Spitfire F XIV.

SPITFIRE XIV

Rolls-Royce had introduced the first of its Griffon series engines at about the same time as the Spitfire IX made its service debut. Boasting larger diameter cylinders and a bigger engine block, the Griffon produced greater power but in its original Mk III version it had only a single-stage supercharger. The airframe initially developed to harness this power was the Mk IV (later re-designated the Mk XX), but a role change for the fighter mid-development saw the once high-altitude optimised Griffon Spitfire altered to achieve its best performance at low level in order to counter Fw 190 'hit and run' raiders that were causing problems along the south coast of England. The resulting Mk XII featured a restyled, longer, engine cowling to house the larger Griffon and clipped 'C' wings for optimum performance 'down low'.

With the airframe employed based closely on the Mk VC, and then the Mk VIII (including the latter aircraft's larger, pointed rudder), the Mk XII had no extra fuel capacity. And with the Griffon being appreciably 'thirstier' than its predecessor, the fighter's range was even worse than the previously short-legged Merlin Spitfire. However, the role for which the Mk XII was used did not require long searching patrols to be flown, and the first of just 100 was delivered to the RAF for two home defence squadrons in February 1943. The Mk XII proved successful in its chosen role, and was also used for shipping reconnaissance and fighter sweeps over France until finally replaced by the vastly improved Mk XIV in September 1944.

The Mk XIV was without a doubt *the* Spitfire that commanded the most respect! The reason for this was simple – the 'state-of-the-art' Griffon 65/66 engine produced almost too much torque for the essentially pre-war design to handle, particularly during take-off. Indeed, a number of early Mk XIV pilots reported that the aircraft felt as if it wanted to 'rotate around the five-bladed propeller', rather the other way round! These longitudinal problems aside, the Spitfire Mk XIV was an awesome fighter to fly thanks to the generous levels of horsepower cranked out by its Griffon engine – 2,050 hp to be precise. Granted, it may have 'put a bit of weight on round the middle', thanks to Supermarine engineers strengthening the essentially Mk VIII fuselage in preparation for the fitment of the new powerplant, but the standard production F XIVE could, nevertheless, attain a top speed of almost 450 mph, and climb to 43,000 ft.

Only 957 production Mk XIVs were built in three variants from January 1944. The standard F XIV had a 'C' wing and 'normal' Spitfire canopy, the F XIVE featured an 'E' wing (with 0.5-in guns replacing the 0.303-in weapons), some of which were clipped for low-level operations, and 'bubble' canopies in late production aircraft, and the FR XIVE was a low-level fighter/tactical reconnaissance version with clipped wings, 'bubble' canopy, oblique camera in the rear fuselage and an additional fuselage fuel tank.

Perhaps the Mk XIV's finest hour came in mid 1944 when its straight-line speed was used to great effect to counter the V-1 menace during Air Defence of Great Britain patrols over southeast England – the Spitfire XIV could outpace all other frontline types, including the Tempest V. A considerable number of Griffon Spitfires were sent to units in the Far East in the last year of the war, although in the most part they arrived too late to see action against the Japanese. A large number of surplus RAF Spitfire XIVs were supplied to the Indian Air Force post-war.

DIMENSIONS AND PERFORMANCE DATA FOR SPITFIRE F XIV

TYPE:	Single-engined monoplane fighter
DIMENSIONS:	Length: 32 ft 8 in (9.96 m)
	Wingspan: 36 ft 10 in (11.23 m)
	Height: 12 ft 8 in (3.86 m)
WEIGHTS:	Empty: 6,600 lb (2,994 kg)
	Max T/O: 9,772 lb (4,433 kg)
PERFORMANCE:	Max Speed: 448 mph (721 km/h)
	Range: 850 miles (1,368 km) with
	two external drop tanks
	Powerplant: Rolls-Royce Griffon 65
	Output: 2,050 hp (1,528 kW)
ARMAMENT:	Two 20 mm cannon and four
	0.303-in machine guns in wings;
	provision for one 500 lb (227 kg)
	or two 250 lb (113 kg) bombs
	externally
FIRST FLIGHT DATE:	January 1943
PRODUCTION:	957

Spitfire LF XVIE.

SPITFIRE XVI

Unlike the numerous Spitfire variants that preceded the Mk XVI, this version of the famous Supermarine design was used principally as a ground-attack aircraft, rather than in its more familiar fighter role. This change in function, if not in form, graphically illustrated that the true versatility of the design had been realised during its long production life.

Initially externally similar in appearance to its more common precursor the Mk IX, the Mk XVI was deemed to warrant a new mark number because it was powered by a fully imported, US-built, Packard Merlin 266 engine. The first Mk XVIs were issued to frontline units in the autumn of 1944, these machines having the traditional high-back fuselage and pointed rudder of late-build LF IXEs – they also boasted two extra fuel tanks in the rear fuselage, as installed in Spitfire IXEs. In response to requests from pilots for better visibility (aviators had complained about the obstructed view back over their shoulders since the first Mk Is entered service in the summer of 1938), a cut-down fuselage version that boasted a bubble canopy was introduced from February 1945.

Thanks to the exceptional power output of the Packard Merlin 266 at low level and the fighter's clipped wings, the Mk XVI became the ideal candidate for ground-attack work in support of the Allied armies fighting their way into Germany. So successful was the aircraft at precision bombing that in the last year of the war, the Spitfire XVI proved to be more usefully employed by the Allies as a dedicated ground-attack aircraft than in its proven day fighter role.

DIMENSIONS AND PERFORMANCE DATA FOR SPITFIRE F XVIE

TYPE:	Single-engined monoplane fighter
DIMENSIONS:	Length: 31 ft 1 in (9.47 m)
	Wingspan: 36 ft 10 in (11.23 m)
	Height: 12 ft 7.75 in (3.86 m)
WEIGHTS:	Empty: 5,800–6,200 lb (2,631–2,812 kg)
	Max T/O: 9,500 lb (4,309 kg)
PERFORMANCE:	Max Speed: 408 mph (657 km/h)
	Range: 980 miles (1,577 km) with external tanks
	Powerplant: Packard Merlin 266
	Output: 1,720 hp (1,282 kW)
ARMAMENT:	Two 20 mm cannon and two 0.5-in machine guns in wings; provision for 1,000 lb (454 kg) bombload externally
FIRST FLIGHT DATE:	mid 1944
PRODUCTION:	1,054

Spitfire FR XVIII.

SPITFIRE XVIII

This variant was further improvement along the lines of the Mks VII, VIII and XIV, and it came into service a little later than the Spitfire Mk 21. In the main it was a Mk XIV with strengthened wings and undercarriage and extra fuel tankage. The extra fuel – 66 Imperial gallons in the fuselage and 26.5 Imperial gallons in each wing – made the fighter useful for reconnaissance, for which role it had alternative F24 or F52 camera installations. Even so, it had the same top speed as the lighter Mk XIV.

The Mk XVIII missed seeing action in World War 2. Although production of the fighter ended in early 1946, it was not until January 1947 that an RAF unit – No 60 Squadron, which was based at Selatar, in Singapore – was re-equipped with the variant. Later, other squadrons in the Far East and Middle East would also receive them. Some 300 F XVIIIs and FR XVIIIs were built, and they saw little action apart from some involvement against guerrillas in the Malayan Emergency. Like the XIV before it, the RIAF/IAF acquired the Spitfire XVIII, 20 ex-RAF examples being ushered into service in 1947.

DIMENSIONS AND PERFORMANCE DATA FOR SPITFIRE F XVIII

TYPE:	Single-engined monoplane fighter
DIMENSIONS:	Length: 32 ft 8 in (9.96 m)
	Wingspan: 36 ft 10 in (11.23 m)
	Height: 12 ft 8 in (3.86 m)
WEIGHTS:	Empty: 6,845 lb (3,104 kg)
	Max T/O: 11,000 lb (4,989 kg)
PERFORMANCE:	Max Speed: 437 mph (703 km/h)
	Range: 850 miles (1,368 km) with
	two external drop tanks
	Powerplant: Rolls-Royce Griffon 67
	Output: 2,375 hp (1,771 kW)
ARMAMENT:	Two 20 mm cannon and two
	0.5-in machine guns in wings;
	provision for three 500 lb (227
	kg) bombs externally
FIRST FLIGHT DATE:	May 1945
PRODUCTION:	300

Spitfire PR XIX.

SPITFIRE PR XIX

Following the usual practice, as soon as Spitfires were available with powerful Griffon 61 series engines, the PRUs made their demands. Still more altitude and a higher top speed suited their needs admirably, but they wanted the advantage of a pressure-cabin which allowed pilots to safely fly the aircraft at altitudes in excess of 40,000 ft. Units had experienced a taste of this with the limited production run PR X (based on the F VII), and they were keen to get hold of the new PR XIX, which evolved from the Spitfire XIV. Boasting a greater range than the PR XI and the cockpit conditions of the PR X, the aeroplane would be broadly similar to the Mk XIV but with modified PR XI wings (more fuel tanks were added) and other modifications associated with the installation of cockpit pressurisation. In general, the latter system was the same as that installed in the Spitfire VII, except that for this aircraft the air intake and blower were on the port side of the engine rather than to starboard.

The camera installation in the PR XIX was broadly similar to that found in the PR XI, with a 'U' fitting provided for either two 'fanned' or a single F52 36-inch vertical camera, two 'fanned' F52 20-inch vertical or two 'fanned' F24 14-inch vertical cameras and one F24 14-inch or 8-inch oblique. In addition, the wing camera installation as used on later PR XIs could be fitted in place on the inter-spar fuel tanks.

The all-up weight of the PR XIX was 7,500 lbs, and with its overall PR blue finish and no guns, the aircraft looked the last word in smooth, purposeful efficiency. Little wonder, then, that the PR XIX was the fastest Spitfire of them all with a top speed of 460 mph – an increase of 100 mph over its elder brother, the Mk I.

DIMENSIONS AND PERFORMANCE DATA FOR SPITFIRE PR XIX

TYPE:	Single-engined monoplane reconnaissance aircraft
DIMENSIONS:	Length: 32 ft 8 in (9.96 m)
	Wingspan: 36 ft 10 in (11.23 m)
	Height: 12 ft 8 in (3.86 m)
WEIGHTS:	Empty: 6,550 lb (2,971 kg)
	Max T/O: 10,450 lb (4,740 kg)
PERFORMANCE:	Max Speed: 460 mph (740 km/h)
	Range: 1,550 miles (2,494 km)
	Powerplant: Rolls-Royce Griffon 66
	Output: 2,035 hp (1,517 kW)
ARMAMENT:	None
FIRST FLIGHT DATE:	April 1944
PRODUCTION:	225

Seafire LF IIIC.

SEAFIRE III

Delayed from reaching production by the RAF's priority on all Spitfire production, the first navalised example did not fly until January 1942 – almost two years after the Royal Navy had enquired about whether a 'Sea Spitfire' could be produced for the Fleet Air Arm. Although not ideally suited to carrier flightdeck operations due to its narrow-track undercarriage and less than robust construction, the Seafire nevertheless provided the Fleet Air Arm with its first truly modern fighter of the conflict. No less than 20 frontline units received Seafires during World War 2, and the aircraft saw action over North Africa, Norway, Sicily, the Normandy beaches, Western Europe and the Far East.

The first aircraft provided to the fleet were ex-RAF Mk VBs, fitted with a vee frame arrestor hook, a strengthened undercarriage and catapult spool. Some 166 Mk VBs were converted into Seafire Mk IBs and delivered between February 1942 and July 1943. The next variant to enter service was the Mk II, which was based on the Mk VC, and retained the latter's non-folding wings. Three sub-variants were built, using different versions of the Merlin engine or incorporating cameras.

From the very beginning the Royal Navy was keen for a folding wing version of the Seafire to be built. The Corsair and Hellcat were due to enter service during the second half of 1943, but competition from the US Navy and US Marine Corps created a degree of uncertainty regarding a secure supply of aircraft. In order to permit

unrestricted frontline service on all of Her Majesty's carriers, the Seafire needed a folding wing. The first production Mk IIC was duly pulled from the production line and used for the development of the folding wing Mk III. The folding system was simple enough, and consisted of one break just inboard of the inner cannon bay and a second at the wing tip. No power-assist folding was ever considered due to weight restrictions, and in the end the new wing added just 125 lbs per aircraft.

It was also at this point that the Seafire would consolidate its armament. This allowed the 'C' wing to be modified internally, with both the outboard cannon bays and the blast-tube stubs being deleted. The Martin-Baker Patent Belt-Fed Mechanism was also adapted. This unit had a lower profile than that of the original, and as a consequence, the large wing blisters over the feed mechanisms were replaced by small teardrop fairings. These two modifications added close to 10 mph to the fighter's top speed.

The F III was also given a different engine – the Merlin 55. It had the same output as the Merlin 45, but was more efficient due to the automatic boost control and barometric governing of the 'full throttle height'. The Merlin 55, along with a cleaner wing and four-bladed propeller, gave the F III an increase of 20 mph at all heights over the Seafire IIC. Between 3,000 ft and 14,000 ft, the Seafire F III was faster than the F6F-3 Hellcat, and was evenly matched with the F4U-1A from

6,000 ft to 10,000 ft. The F III was designed to fight at heights between 8,000 ft and 15,000 ft, thus making it a true medium level fighter.

First flown in the autumn of 1943, the L III version of the Seafire would be produced in the greatest numbers. The logical successor to the L IIC, the new version was identical to the F III except that it was powered by the Merlin 55M engine. While the latter had slightly less power than the Merlin 32 (1,585 hp for the 55M at 2,750 ft, versus 1,640hp at 1,750 ft for the 32), the new L III was actually faster in level flight. The fastest of all the Merlin-engined Seafires, the L Mk III was capable of 358 mph at 6,000 ft, and in 1945 it was still the fastest and steepest climbing Allied carrier interceptor. Later production L IIIs received the Hispano Mk V cannon. This was a lighter weapon with a shorter barrel. The final version of the L III was the FR III. It was basically the same as the LR IIC, but with a slight difference in the camera installation.

DIMENSIONS AND PERFORMANCE DATA FOR SEAFIRE F III

TYPE:	Single-engined monoplane fighter
DIMENSIONS:	Length: 30 ft 2.5 in (9.21 m)
	Wingspan: 36 ft 10 in (11.23 m)
	Height: 11 ft 5.5 in (3.49 m)
WEIGHTS:	Empty: 6,204 lb (2,814 kg)
	Loaded Weight: 7,640 lb (3,465 kg)
PERFORMANCE:	Max Speed: 348 mph (560 km/h)
	Range: 725 miles (1,167 km) with external tank
	Powerplant: Rolls-Royce Merlin 55
	Output: 1,470 hp (1,096 kW)
ARMAMENT:	Two 20 mm cannon and four 0.303-in machine guns in wings; provision for one 500 lb (227 kg) or two 250 lb (113 kg) bombs externally
FIRST FLIGHT DATE:	7 January 1942
PRODUCTION:	1,163 (all Seafire III variants)

Seafire F XVII.

SEAFIRE XVII

The Fleet Air Arm had expressed an interest in acquiring a Griffon-powered Seafire in early 1943, and in March of the following year then Lieutenant Commander Eric Brown commenced carrier flightdeck trials with the prototype Seafire XV aboard HMS *Indefatigable*. The Mk XV utilised an L III airframe to which had been added the wing-root fuel tanks of the Spitfire IX and the retractable tailwheel and enlarged vertical surfaces of the Spitfire VIII. The fighter was powered by the naval version of the Griffon engine, the Mk VI.

The Seafire XV entered service shortly after World War 2 had ended, and by then the improved Mk XVII was under development. With similar dimensions to the previous mark, this aeroplane was the first Seafire variant to incorporate the 'bubble' canopy. The larger rudder and faired 'sting' arrestor hook of the Mk XV were also incorporated into the Seafire XVII, as was the provision for carrying underwing bombs. Another innovation exclusive to this mark was the ability to employ Rocket-Assisted Take-Off Gear (RATOG). This catered for the fitting, on each side of the fuselage at the root end of the wing, of a carrier to hold two rocket motors. The aircraft's electrical system (upgraded from 12 volts to 24 volts in the Seafire XVII) was adapted to fire the rockets. The carriers could be jettisoned after take-off, thus leaving the aeroplane unencumbered by ancillary fittings. The rockets burned for approximately four seconds, and the take-off run was considerably reduced by their impetus.

Once in fleet service, Seafire XVIIs never used RATOG at sea unless ranged forward of the first crash barrier on the flightdeck. This was because of the excessive torque swing to starboard created by the Griffon engine when opened up for take-off.

With the Seafire XVII, the Royal Navy at last had an aircraft capable of almost 400 mph in level flight. At the other end of the speed range, the deck-landing characteristics of the aeroplane were improved by the incorporation of a long-stroke undercarriage, which provided a full travel of eight inches against the normal stroke of less than five inches. The new undercarriage was significantly stronger and, therefore, less likely to break under the strain. The increased oleo stroke also provided greater propeller clearance on the deck, and thus markedly reduced the Seafire's propensity to 'peck'

(the blade tips hitting the deck during arresting), it also offered a lower rebound ratio. This reduced the bounce that had carried Seafires fitted with the earlier undercarriage over the arrestor wires and into the crash barrier.

Although the F XVII was an improvement over the F XV, it was still viewed by the Fleet Air Arm as an interim model pending availability of a Seafire fitted with a two-stage Griffon 60 series engine and six-bladed contra-rotating propellers.

DIMENSIONS AND PERFORMANCE DATA FOR SEAFIRE F XVII

TYPE:	Single-engined monoplane fighter
DIMENSIONS:	Length: 32 ft 3 in (9.83 m)
	Wingspan: 36 ft 10 in (11.23 m)
	Height: 14 ft 1 in (4.65 m)
WEIGHTS:	Empty: 6,385 lb (2,895 kg)
	Max T/O: 8,150 lb (3,695 kg)
PERFORMANCE:	Max Speed: 392 mph (630 km/h)
	Range: 435 miles (700 km)
	Powerplant: Rolls-Royce Griffon VI
	Output: 1,850 hp (1,379 kW)
ARMAMENT:	Two 20 mm cannon and four 0.303-in machine guns in wings; provision for three 500 lb (227 kg) bombs externally
FIRST FLIGHT DATE:	Late 1944
PRODUCTION:	234

BIBLIOGRAPHY

Bowyer, Michael, *Fighting Colours*, PSL, 1969

Brown, Eric, *Seafire – From The Cockpit 13*, Ad Hoc Publications, 2010

Deere, Air Commodore Alan, *Nine Lives*, Wingham Press, 1991

Dibbs, John and Holmes, Tony, *Spitfire – Flying Legend*, Osprey Publishing, 1996

Duke, Neville, *Test Pilot*, Grub Street, 1992

Flintham, Vic and Thomas, Andrew, *Combat Codes*, Airlife, 2003

Franks, Norman (editor), *The War Diaries of Neville Duke*, Grub Street, 1995

Franks, Norman L. R., *Royal Air Force Fighter Command Losses of the Second World War – Volume 1 Operational Losses: Aircraft and Crews 1939–1941*, Midland Publishing Ltd, 2008

Franks, Norman L. R., *Royal Air Force Fighter Command Losses of the Second World War – Volume 2 Operational Losses: Aircraft and Crews 1942–1943*, Midland Publishing Ltd, 1998

Goulding, James and Jones, Robert, *Camouflage & Markings – RAF Fighter Command Northern Europe 1936 to 1945*, Ducimus Books Limited, 1970

Holmes, Tony, *Jane's Pocket Guide to Fighters of World War 2*, HarperCollins, 1999

Holmes, Tony, *USAAF Colours 1 – American Eagles*, Classic Publications, 2001

Holmes, Tony, *Duel 5 – Spitfire vs Bf 109*, Osprey Publishing, 2007

Jefford, Wing Commander C. G., *RAF Squadrons*, Airlife, 2001

Johnson, 'Johnnie', *Wing Leader*, Chatto & Windus, 1956

Matusiak, Wojtek and Grudzien, Robert, *Aircraft of the Aces 127 – Polish Spitfire Aces*, Osprey Publishing, 2015

Morgan, Eric B. and Shacklady, Edward, *Spitfire – The History*, Key Publishing, 1987

Nijboer, Donald, *Aviation Elite Units 35 – No 126 Wing RCAF*, Osprey Publishing, 2010

Nijboer, Donald, *Duel 16 – Seafire vs A6M Zero*, Osprey Publishing, 2009

Nijboer, Donald, *Duel 60 – Spitfire V vs C.202 Folgore*, Osprey Publishing, 2014

Price, Alfred, *Spitfire – A Complete Fighting History*, PRC Ltd, 1991

Quill, Jeffrey, *Spitfire*, Arrow Books, 1983

Rawlings, John, *Fighter Squadrons of the RAF and their Aircraft*, MacDonald, 1969

Riley, Gordon, Arnold, Peter and Trant, Graham, *Spitfire Survivors Then and Now – Volume I Mks I to XII*, A-Eleven Publications, 2010

Riley, Gordon, Arnold, Peter and Trant, Graham, *Spitfire Survivors Then and Now – Volume 2 Mks XIV to F 24 plus Seafires*, A-Eleven Publications, 2013

Sarkar, Dilip, *Spitfire Squadron*, Air Research, 1990

Shores, Christopher and Williams, Clive, *Aces High*, Grub Street, 1994

Shores, Christopher, *Those Other Eagles*, Grub Street, 2004

Singh, Vikram, *Spitfires in the Sun*, United Services Institute, 2014

Smallwood, Hugh, *Spitfire in Blue*, Osprey Publishing, 1996

Thomas, Andrew, *Aircraft of the Aces 81 – Griffon Spitfire Aces*, Osprey Publishing, 2008

Thomas, Andrew, *Aircraft of the Aces 87 – Spitfire Aces of Burma and the Pacific*, Osprey Publishing, 2009

Townshend Bickers, Richard, *Ginger Lacey – Fighter Pilot*, Pan, 1969

Wynn, Kenneth G., *Men of the Battle of Britain*, Frontline Books, 2015

INDEX